I0414030

Editor-in-Chief and Founder:
   Lyndon H. LaRouche, Jr.
Editorial Board: *Lyndon H. LaRouche, Jr. , Helga
   Zepp-LaRouche, Robert Ingraham, Tony
   Papert, Gerald Rose, Dennis Small, Jeffrey
   Steinberg, William Wertz*
Co-Editors: *Robert Ingraham, Tony Papert*
Managing Editor: *Nancy Spannaus*
Technology: *Marsha Freeman*
Books: *Katherine Notley*
Ebooks: *Richard Burden*
Graphics: *Alan Yue*
Photos: *Stuart Lewis*
Circulation Manager: *Stanley Ezrol*

INTELLIGENCE DIRECTORS
Counterintelligence: *Jeffrey Steinberg, Michele
   Steinberg*
Economics: *John Hoefle, Marcia Merry Baker,
   Paul Gallagher*
History: *Anton Chaitkin*
Ibero-America: *Dennis Small*
Russia and Eastern Europe: *Rachel Douglas*
United States: *Debra Freeman*

INTERNATIONAL BUREAUS
Bogotá: *Miriam Redondo*
Berlin: *Rainer Apel*
Copenhagen: *Tom Gillesberg*
Houston: *Harley Schlanger*
Lima: *Sara Madueño*
Melbourne: *Robert Barwick*
Mexico City: *Gerardo Castilleja Chávez*
New Delhi: *Ramtanu Maitra*
Paris: *Christine Bierre*
Stockholm: *Ulf Sandmark*
United Nations, N.Y.C.: *Leni Rubinstein*
Washington, D.C.: *William Jones*
Wiesbaden: *Göran Haglund*

ON THE WEB
e-mail: eirns@larouchepub.com
www.larouchepub.com
www.executiveintelligencereview.com
www.larouchepub.com/eiw
Webmaster: *John Sigerson*
Assistant Webmaster: *George Hollis*
Editor, Arabic-language edition: *Hussein Askary*

EIR (ISSN 0273-6314) *is published weekly
(50 issues), by EIR News Service, Inc.,
P.O. Box 17390, Washington, D.C. 20041-0390.
(703) 297-8434*

European Headquarters: E.I.R. GmbH, Postfach
Bahnstrasse 9a, D-65205, Wiesbaden, Germany
Tel: 49-611-73650
Homepage: http://www.eir.de
e-mail: info@eir.de
Director: Georg Neudecker

Montreal, Canada: 514-461-1557
eir@eircanada.ca

Denmark: EIR - Danmark, Sankt Knuds Vej 11,
basement left, DK-1903 Frederiksberg, Denmark.
Tel.: +45 35 43 60 40, Fax: +45 35 43 87 57. e-mail:
eirdk@hotmail.com.

Mexico City: EIR, Sor Juana Inés de la Cruz 242-2
Col. Agricultura C.P. 11360
Delegación M. Hidalgo, México D.F.
Tel. (5525) 5318-2301
eirmexico@gmail.com

Canada Post Publication Sales Agreement
#40683579

Postmaster: Send all address changes to *EIR*, P.O.
Box 17390, Washington, D.C. 20041-0390.

Signed articles in *EIR* represent the views of the authors,
and not necessarily those of the Editorial Board.

The New Stage of Human Evolution

EDITORIAL

Helga Zepp-LaRouche: The World Looks Much Different from China

June 1—*Schiller Institute founder and President Helga Zepp-LaRouche has just completed a major trip to China, which began with her participation in the May 14-15 Belt and Road Forum for International Cooperation in Beijing. She gave the following briefing today to her American associates, which is also posted on the* LaRouche PAC *website.*

I want to make sure that you get a first impression of my trip from me, because I think the worst mistake we could make would be to respond to the absolutely incredible psywar propaganda coming from the U.S. mainstream media and the neoliberal media in Europe, such as *Spiegel Online*, with its Chief Editor's piece which was *really* out of this way! It is very clear that people who are primarily relying on such media have a completely, totally, 100% wrong idea of what the reality is, of what's going on. And we should really get that out of our heads and not try to swim within the bounds of a fishbowl that is an artificially created environment. Because, from my standpoint, the world looks very, very different.

First of all, I have said this already, and I reiterate it: With the Belt and Road Forum, the world has dramatically consolidated the beginning of the new era, and I don't think at all, that—short of World War III—this is going to go away, because the majority of the world is moving in a completely liberated way. And first of all, this was the highest level conference I have ever participated in. There were 28 heads of state, speaking one after the other, and obviously, the speech by Xi Jinping was absolutely outstanding. Whoever has time to listen to it, should do so, because it was a very, very Confu-

cian speech, which set the tone for the two-day conference in a very clear way. So, please listen to it when you have some time.

To understand what is going on, you have to think what this organization, and Lyn [LaRouche] in particular, has done for the last, almost 50 years. In 1971 Lyn recognized, for the first time, what the significance of the dismantling of the Bretton Woods system was. Consider all of the many, many things we have done in the more than 40 years since then. Lyn came back from the Iraqi Ba'ath Party celebration in 1975 and then proposed the International Development Bank (IDB) to foster a new world economic order. For one year we campaigned with this IDB proposal which then basically became part of the Colombo, Sri Lanka resolution of the Non-Aligned Movement in 1976. Then, at the end of the 1970s, we worked with Indira Gandhi on a 40-year development plan for India.

In 1976, we published a book on the industrialization of Africa. We worked with Mexican President José López Portillo on "Operation Juárez." We put out a fifty-year Pacific Basin development plan. Lyn proposed the Oasis Plan for developing the Middle East, in 1975. And then, naturally, when the Berlin Wall came down and the Soviet Union disintegrated, we proposed the Productive Triangle and the Eurasian Land-Bridge. All of these proposals!

And just think of the many, many activities we carried out, conferences all over five continents, all of this was on the level of ideas, on the level of program. But only when Xi Jinping put the New Silk Road on the agenda in 2013—and in the subsequent four years of breathtaking developments of the One Belt, One Road

CGTN

Dr. Su Ge (left) and Helga Zepp-LaRouche (center) were interviewed by Yang Rui (right) on his CGTN Dialogue show, May 15, 2017.

Forget the media! Forget these whores in the press who are really just prostitutes for the British Empire. Don't pay any attention to what they say, and don't allow the people you are talking to, to do it either.

When Trump promised $1 trillion infrastructure investments, this was the right thing, and we put out the right program saying the United States must join the Silk Road, *and that should be our focus* and nothing else. Everything else should be a subsumed aspect of that. This is the strategically important thing, and when the head of the China Investment Corporation (CIC), Ding Xuedong, said it's not $1 trillion but $8 trillion that the United States needs, he was absolutely on the mark; you know it yourself from the condition of the roads other infrastructure in all of the United States.

initiative—have these ideas begun to be realized! And now the genie is out of the bottle!

LaRouche, China, Trump

Now you have the Bi-Oceanic Railway discussion and the tunnels and bridges connecting the Atlantic and Pacific in Latin America, and railways are now being opened up in Africa—this is unprecedented! This was not done by the IMF or the World Bank. They suppressed it with their conditionalities. But with the Asian Infrastructure Investment Bank (AIIB), the New Development Bank of the BRICS, the New Silk Road Fund, the Maritime Silk Road Fund, the direct investment of the China Exim Bank, the Bank of China—all of these projects are now proceeding, and they have completely changed the attitude and the built the self-confidence of all participating countries.

The way people in China look at President Trump is absolutely different from what the western media are trying to say. They are very positive about Trump, in the same way that people in Russia think that Trump is somebody you can absolutely have a decent relationship with, and that is reality.

The fact that the CIC has now set up an office in New York, advising Chinese investors on investing in the United States, and vice versa, helping U.S. investors to invest in China; the fact that the Chinese are invited to participate in this infrastructure conference in June, all of this is absolutely going in the right direction.

What happened at the Belt and Road Forum and the many meetings I had afterwards,— after all, I spent two full weeks in Beijing, in Nanjing, in Shanghai—many of these things I'm not reporting on, because they're just works in progress. But in the many interviews, many published quotes, and the general view—you can ask Kasia Kruczkowski and Stefan Tolksdorf, or Bill Jones—we were treated with the highest possible respect. People are fully aware of Lyn's significance as a theoretician of physical economy, his ideas are highly respected, and people treated me as we should be treated, namely as people who have devoted their entire lives to the common good of humanity. And this is absolutely in stark contrast to the shitty behavior that we are normally getting from the neoliberals in the trans-Atlantic region.

Stay On the Offensive!

You should understand what the attack on Trump is supposed to do: It is to make it difficult for him to focus on the positive tasks, and there are quite a number of them—including his working relationship with Russia and China—that are strategically most important. So instead, he has to defend himself, and everybody thinks they have to spend all their time defending themselves. Just think back, for those of you who were around then, how *our* lives as an organization changed with the attack in 1986. Up to that point, we were all positive, we were winning primaries in Illinois, we were thinking in terms of creating three private universities because we had a network of around a hundred professors who wanted to implement Lyn's ideas in the form of a curriculum in universities.

And then, after the attack came in 1986, carried out by the same apparatus that is now going after Trump, we had to spend all this money on lawyers, and we had to defend ourselves, and it changed the life of the organization completely, and that's what they're trying to do to Trump!

So don't fall for it. The idea that we are losing is *completely* off! Mankind is on the winning track, and we have to pull the American people up, bring the American people into this, to create the kind of ferment necessary to ensure that the infrastructure program, as a first step, is on the agenda, and on everybody's mind, and nothing else.

I just wanted to say that because from the initial discussions I had today, I got the impression that people are much too underneath it, and even if Europe is still in the grip of the EU Commission, I mean, if Merkel wants to be the leader of the free West,— forget it. Macron just had an excellent meeting with Putin, defining a cordial relationship with Russia! This is not what Merkel and Obama have been cooking up—for example, when Obama addressed the *Kirchentag*, the Protestant Church Assembly in Berlin on May 25. But Merkel is pretty isolated.

Just look around Europe: French President Emmanuel Macron sends Jean-Pierre Raffarin, the former Prime Minister, to the Belt and Road Forum, and he gave an excellent speech on why China and France must work together. Italian Prime Minister Paolo Gentiloni said China and Italy will work together on the development of Africa. All of the East Europeans—Tsipras of Greece, Serbia, Hungary, Czechia's Zeman, Orban of Hungary—all of them were absolutely enthusiastic about the Belt and Road Initiative. And now even Germany—it shows that German industry is actually getting it, that their interest is to work on joint ventures in third countries together with China. So I think even Germany will change.

I have a strong conviction that by the end of this year, it will look completely different, because the development perspective is so contagious, that I think all the efforts of the British Empire to somehow throw in a monkey wrench, will not work!

So take the winning perspective, take the high ground, think strategically. And realize that what is happening in reality, in many, many development projects around the world, is what this organization has been fighting for, for almost half a century. The worst thing we could do would be to look at it from inside the United States, from within the box, when the whole world has moved out of the box decisively, with the Belt and Road Forum, which is not going to be stopped by anything.

EIR Contents

www.larouchepub.com Volume 44, Number 23, June 9, 2017

Cover This Week

I. The Real Issues of the Economy

EXCELLENT! NOW FUSION, NEW SILK ROAD

President Trump Dumps Paris Climate Accord

by Benjamin Deniston

June 3—The following is an edited transcript of a presentation by Benjamin Deniston, delivered on the June 2, 2017 LaRouche PAC Friday Webcast.

President Trump's announcement that the United States is going to pull out of the Paris Climate Accord is a really big deal; this is excellent. To my knowledge, this is the first U.S. President who has actually kicked back against this whole climate change scare in a serious way. The Clinton Administration pushed it; despite the narrative of this being a Republican versus Democrat issue, the George W. Bush Administration went along with the broader program, as with the insane biofuels program, for example; and Obama pushed it big time. Now, we finally have a President who is actually kicking back against this.

This is very important. Trump deserves respect and support for fighting against this climate change scare, because this isn't just some policy issue, this decision is confronting a coordinated global campaign run by the highest levels of the Anglo-Dutch oligarchy. Now we have the chance to end this Malthusian program and get back to growth and development, if President Trump can follow this up by joining the new global development paradigm being led by China's New Silk Road development policy.

Economics

It was important that Trump highlighted the economic effects of CO_2 reduction schemes during his announcement. Some try to limit the discussion to an academic debate, but there is the reality of the manner in which this is affecting the general population. What's the effect on your citizens of going with these policies?

They say CO_2 is terrible, it's a pollutant, and therefore, we must to go with all these wonderful, clean energy solutions. They paint this rosy picture about green energy, when in fact it has devastating effects on the real-life conditions of our population. This whole Green energy narrative is ridiculous.

If you want to talk about the reduction in CO_2 emissions and the Green energy programs, look at what Germany is facing in terms of their energy prices. This is an important case study in what happens when you massively subsidize wind and solar, while abandoning nuclear and reducing fossil fuels. In Germany, between 2004 and 2015, their energy prices went up 50%, from $0.23 cents a kilowatt-hour in U.S. values, to $0.35 cents a kilowatt-hour. They were already, in 2004, twice the rate we pay in the United States on average. But over that ten-year period—driven by CO_2-reduction efforts, green energy, and then the nuclear exit—prices went up another 50%, to three times what Americans pay on average for energy. What does this mean for your economy? For your industry? For your poorer population? This has already been driving industries to leave Germany.

In 2013, just one subsidy in Germany—a major surcharge added to residential power bills to pay for wind and solar—was the equivalent of $0.07 per kilowatt-hour. That alone is 60% of what we pay on average in the United States. This is just for one subsidy, just for wind and solar.

This surcharge is before the massive, extra expense of new transmission systems, battery banks, and related aspects of a so-called "smart grid" infrastructure system (needed to handle the irregular surges and collapses inherent in wind and solar) are added.

Most importantly, these cost values are shadows of

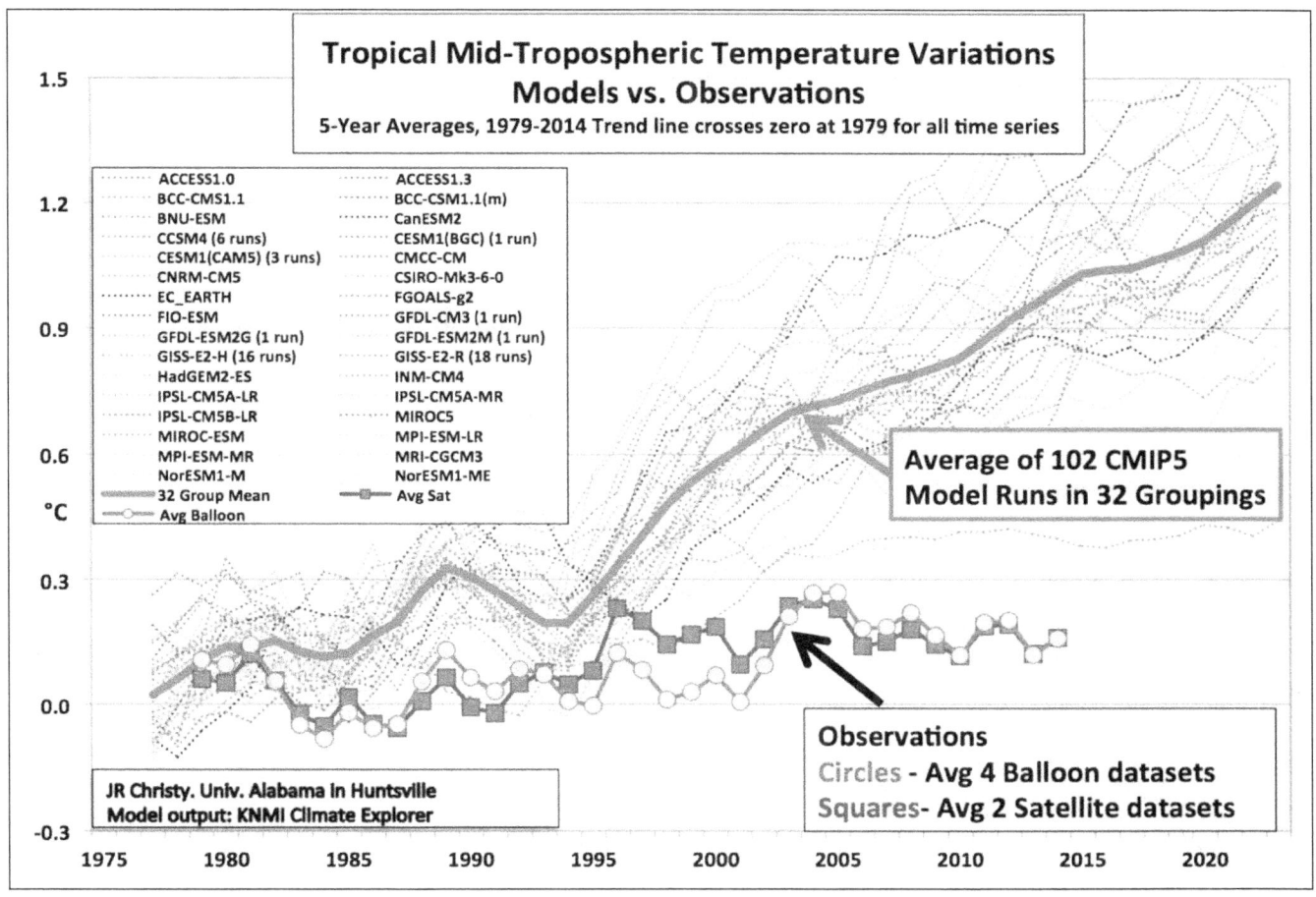

Tropical Mid-Tropospheric Temperature Variations
Models vs. Observations
5-Year Averages, 1979-2014 Trend line crosses zero at 1979 for all time series

Average of 102 CMIP5 Model Runs in 32 Groupings

Observations
Circles - Avg 4 Balloon datasets
Squares- Avg 2 Satellite datasets

JR Christy. Univ. Alabama In Huntsville
Model output: KNMI Climate Explorer

John Christy, Professor of Atmospheric Science and State Climatologist at the National Space Science and Technology Center, University of Alabama, Huntsville, Alabama; presented at a May 13, 2015 House Committee on Natural Resources hearing.

a physical principle: LaRouche's metric of energy flux-density. Human progress is characterized by increases in energy flux-density, associated with fuels with higher energy densities and new domains of physical chemistry.

The idea that we can transition to some wonderful world powered by wind and solar electricity is a farce; it's a fraud. These power sources inherently have a lower energy density, necessitating a higher physical cost to society per unit of power supplied. We need to go in the other direction, and to the degree necessary, use oil, coal, and gas in the context of existing infrastructure systems, while rapidly developing the more advanced, higher forms of energy such as nuclear fission and fusion—that's really the future. The future is increasing energy use per capita, increasing the use of higher qualities of energy per capita.

What Does CO_2 Not Do?

Secondly, in the context of the freakout reaction to Trump's exiting from the Paris Accord, it's worth re-examining the issue of rising atmospheric CO_2 levels. What does CO_2 do? It's now officially labeled a pollutant by the EPA, and the media bombards you with claims that it will cause disastrous, extreme weather, catastrophic climate change, flood our cities with sea-level rise, and create a mass extinction of species. All bunk.

A lot could be said, but let's just highlight one study, comparing 32 different climate models' predictions of the effects of CO_2 increase, with the reality that's happened just in the last couple of decades.

The many thin dotted lines [in the graph above] are what these computer models predict for temperature rise due to CO_2 increases, and the thick red line is their average prediction (based on a run from 1979). But compare that to the actual observations indicated in the blue and green lines (the squares and the dots). You see that none of the computer models have been accurate in predicting what actually happened. Satellite measurements derived from two different assessments, as well as independent *in situ* measurements with balloon systems, have shown that the temperature over the past 15 years has been relatively flat with little or no increase—despite the largest increases in CO_2 levels in recorded human history. *None* of the models predicted this global temperature flatline, they all predicted significant global temperature rise (as a response to the CO_2 increase). So, have this in mind when you hear these scare stories about CO_2 increase being some terrible thing. They're basing it all on these models that have already been shown to be ridiculous.

What Does CO_2 Actually Do?

But there's another interesting aspect to the CO_2 issue, which isn't discussed at all. Apparently, it's a secret for many of these fear-mongering climate change pundits, that CO_2 is actually a critical part of the biosphere. People talk about being "pro-green"—CO_2 is totally pro-green, it's as green as you get!

A few weeks back I had the opportunity to interview a scientist who has reviewed and consolidated thousands of studies showing the positive effects of higher CO_2 levels on plant life. Dr. Craig Idso is the Founder of the Center for the Study of Carbon Dioxide and Global Change, and a member of CO_2 Coalition.

His work covers controlled experiments with greenhouses (studying different plant species at different CO_2 levels), assessments of the implications of this for agriculture, and satellite measurements of regional and global biospheric activity.

The results of these studies are remarkable and speak for themselves. According to global satellite measurements, over the past 35 years the entire biosphere has seen a 6% to 15% increase in total plant biomass production. We're not talking about a 10th of a percent or a half of a percent, but 6% to 15% for the entire globe; that's huge.

Based on the controlled greenhouse studies, Dr. Idso has been able to determine that the rising CO_2 levels in recent decades have increased agricultural crop yields by over $3 trillion—more food and more efficient agriculture production.

And another benefit—which is a big irony, in a certain sense—is the effects of higher CO_2 levels on plant water use efficiency. You actually get a highly significant boost for certain plant species in their ability to produce more biomass with less water use. This has rather interesting implications for drier regions in particular, where water is the limiting factor in plant growth. And now, all of a sudden, with higher concentrations of plant food in the atmosphere, CO_2, they can grow in regions they couldn't grow in before; they can be healthier in regions they couldn't be healthy in before. And you just take a look at places we've had water issues—like California—and we have our crazy governor in California, running around pretending he's the world leader on CO_2, when his state is actually benefiting from the fact there's been higher CO_2 levels in the context of the recent droughts. The ironies are just all over the place.

A Top-Down, Imperial Policy

You've really got to ask yourself, why are none of these basic scientific facts even being added into the discussion about effects of CO_2 rise? All you hear are these flimsy scare stories, presented by the media as if they were scientific facts, but basic, unambiguous scientific data and studies demonstrating the positive effects of CO_2 rise are completely left out of the discussion. People need to let that irony sink in.

Let's talk about reality. For decades, Helga and Lyndon LaRouche have warned you, the whole global warming issue is not really about global warming. That's just the latest scare story certain people have grabbed onto and pushed to bolster a Malthusian ideology (before global warming it was ozone holes, and overpopulation, and global cooling).

In 2015 *Executive Intelligence Review* released an updated report exposing the forces pushing this climate change scare, "Global Warming Scare Is Population Reduction, Not Science," which details the origins, not just of the climate-change scare, but more broadly, of this whole environmentalist movement, demonstrating that it comes from an oligarchical, Malthusian ideology. Look at the climate issue in that context.

Just look at the founders of the modern environmentalist movement, the people who created the entire structure that pushed this whole environmentalist movement globally. Just highlight the top figures: Sir Julian Huxley, a lifelong proponent of eugenics, who was head of the British Eugenics Society. After World War II, after Hitler's horrific war crimes and crimes against humanity were exposed, along with their connection to eugenics, Huxley still promoted eugenics in his position in the UN, as the head of UNESCO at the time. Prince Philip, whenever he gets the chance, talks about how terrible population growth is, and the fact that population growth is the number one problem on the planet. He has said that if he could be reincarnated,

Dr. Craig Idso, Carbon Dioxide Specialist

June 3—Below are excerpts from a March 23, 2017 interview with Dr. Craig Idso, conducted at the Heartland Institute's 12th International Conference on Climate Change (ICCC-12). Dr. Idso is the founder of the Center for the Study of Carbon Dioxide and Global Change. He is a member of the American Association for the Advancement of Science; of the American Geophysical Union; of the American Meteorological Society; and of the CO_2 Coalition.

Dr. Craig Idso

Dr. Craig Idso: There are three main benefits which result from increasing carbon dioxide concentrations in the atmosphere: The first is that it increases plant productivity for biomass of the plant. On average, what we see is that for a doubling of CO_2, something that's going to happen by the end of this century, most are herbaceous plants, non-woody plants like crops and things like that, will experience anywhere from a 25% to a 55% increase in biomass per yield. And that's a phenomenal result and that's something that's going to happen just because we raise the CO_2 concentration and nothing else. . . .

Second is that higher CO_2 concentrations help increase the plant's water use efficiency. Again, a doubling of CO_2 allows plants to use about half as much water as they need to produce the same amount of tissue, so that is another phenomenal benefit.

And then the third benefit is that higher CO_2 concentrations help to ameliorate environmental stresses. So if you have a stress from hot air temperature, maybe low light, low levels of soil fertility, those sorts of things, if you have higher CO_2 concentrations, the higher levels tend to reduce or lessen that stress, if not completely ameliorate it under a doubling of CO_2.

You put all those three benefits together, and what you get is a tremendous benefit to the biosphere, to the growth. And we're seeing that already: We see it in tree-ring cores, you can look at how their water use efficiency has improved over time, and we see anywhere from 35% to 40% increase already, as the CO_2 concentration has increased by about 40%. . . .

So the satellites have been up measuring reflectivity of vegetation, over the entire globe ever since about the early 1980s. And what they find consistently, whether they're focusing on a particular region of the globe or the globe as a whole, you get anywhere from about 6% to 15% increase in biomass in that period of time. . . . The globe as a whole, or in total, is actually in a better off condition now than it was when those measurements began. . . .

I did the first approximation to determine what is the net monetary benefit on crop production globally, in the past and then also projected into the future, and what I found was that over the 50-year period from 1961 to 2011, it amounts to about $3.2 trillion on the global economy, a phenomenal benefit. And then, projecting that forward in time, as the CO_2 concentration is going to continue to rise, from about 2012 to 2050, we expect it to be about $10 trillion to the economy.

And that's just really scratching the surface, because you could look at studies—for example, I'll take rice, where there's a number of genotypes of rice, and scientists have looked at, for example—in one study I'm thinking of—they looked at 16 different genotypes of rice, and how those genotypes responded to a doubling of CO_2, and they received values that ranged from about zero all the way to a whopping 265%. So, if governments and scientists focused on those specific genotypes that we received the greatest increase in biomass per unit of CO_2 rise, and then grew them, we could have this phenomenal increase in agriculture and have no problem in feeding the planet in the future.

he'd like to come back as a deadly virus to reduce world population. That's his view, that's his belief-system. Prince Bernhard of the Netherlands was actually a Nazi, and then worked for Nazi intelligence (and there are credible accusations that he helped Nazi war criminals escape after World War II).

These people came together and started the environmentalist movement in the immediate post-World War II period, and in the '50s and '60s it started to take off. This is the ideology behind this. It's not about the debates you see on the media, about this claim or that claim on supposed science of CO_2. If you really want to understand the issue, it's this oligarchical, Malthusian ideology that's been campaigning for generations against economic development, against population growth, against the development of so-called Third

---

The Founding Fathers of the Environmentalist Movement

Prince Philip
- 1930s—His siblings married into pro-NAZI aristocratic families in Germany.
- 1933—He studied under the NAZI race-science curriculum in Germany.
- Late 1930s—He maintained a secretive relation with the pro-NAZI king of England (Edward VIII) after the king was forced to abdicate.

Prince Philip

- 1961—He became the United Kingdom President of the World Wildlife Fund from 1961 to 1982.
- 1981—He was president of International World Wildlife Fund 1981-1996.
- 1996—He became President Emeritus of the World Wildlife Fund.

Sir Julian Huxley
- 1937—He was vice-president of the British Eugenics Society 1937 to 1944.
- 1948—After the world was exposed to the horrors of Hitler's eugenics program, Huxley continued to promote the development of eugenics as the first director of UNESCO (placing a call in support of eugenics in UNESCO's founding document).
- 1958—He became Sir Julian Huxley upon being knighted by the Queen.
- 1959—He was president of the British Eugenics Society from 1959 to 1962.
- 1961—He was a co-founder of World Wildlife Fund.

Sir Julian Huxley

Prince Bernhard
- 1930s—He was a member of the Nazi SS, then worked with a special Nazi SS Intelligence Unit in IG Farbenindustrie. The Nazi concentration camp/slave-labor system was later pioneered there.
- 1936—He resigned from Nazi SS to marry the future Queen Juliana, signing his resignation, "Heil Hitler!" Hitler sent congratulations to their wedding.
- 1940s—He was director of KLM airlines during the time that the airlines were covertly flying Nazi war criminals out of Germany and into Argentina to escape prosecution,

Prince Bernhard

- 1961—He was co-founder of the World Wildlife Fund.
- 1961-1976—He was president of the World Wildlife Fund.
- 1970—He founded "The 1001: A Nature Trust" to organize financial support for the funding of the environmentalist movement.

World nations. These are people who have said we cannot allow the world to rise to the living standards of America and the West. Think of Obama traveling to Africa, telling students in Africa, if you all had air conditioning and cars the planet would boil over, so that's not an option for you.

Dump the Past, Get into the Future

And that's the issue. Despite what many may believe, the Paris Climate Accord is an expression of the old Malthusian, geopolitical paradigm—it's the past—and what we're seeing emerging with everything around China's New Silk Road/Belt and Road Initiative (and its recent breakthrough leadership forum) is the future. So Trump's dumping of this climate change issue is completely coherent with the fight to get the United States to break from this old geopolitical, zero-sum game, Malthusian paradigm, and get into building the future again.

Energy is certainly critical. Mr. LaRouche has defined the next steps: Concentrate on fusion and on nuclear fission as needed for the time being. The key is not only utilizing existing infrastructure for energy sources such as coal and natural gas, but developing the future energy sources that are going to do much more than allow moderate growth in energy use. What kind of energy production will enable nations around the world to come up to the same per capita energy use that we have in the United States now? What will support even higher levels, including in the United States? How can we dramatically increase the total energy-flux density of the entire global economy? That's the future. The entire history of the development of mankind has always been intimately connected with, and tied to these kinds of increases in energy-flux density. That's got to be the next step in development.

With China's Belt and Road Initiative, the world is moving in that direction, and if the U.S.A. joins that process, we can secure this shift—this can't be stressed enough. We are on the verge of a global, historical paradigm shift, this provides the perspective of the end of a geopolitical system. We have to get Americans to understand the depth of this ongoing revolution, and the importance of the United States jumping on board with this, immediately. If you now get the United States on board with Russia and China, and the nations allied with them, that's it. We can have the future, we can create the future we want with that alliance.

A Future Platform of U.S. Infrastructure

by Jason Ross

June 6—New York City, the economic, cultural, and intellectual capital of the United States, is an infrastructure disaster! At key choke points in the region's infrastructure network, commuters and travelers pass through tunnels built when the oldest people alive today were born. Continual disruptions plague the overcrowded subway system, which now suffers 70,000 delays per month, compared to 28,000 in 2012. In March and April, major train derailments at Penn Station, the busiest rail station in the western hemisphere, resulted in four days of partial closures, delaying over one million commutes. The planned shutdown of two, century-old tunnels across the East River portends a "Summer of Hell" this July and August, to be followed by the planned shutdown of a key subway line, currently serving a quarter-million passengers, during 2019-2020. Were one of the century-old, cross-Hudson tunnels leading into Penn Station to fail, the quarter-million New Jersey residents they currently bring to New York would be faced with a capacity of 60,000 or less. How could America's greatest city be in such poor condition?

And yet, while New York stands out as a stunning case study, the problems seen there are not unique. They are symptomatic of the profoundly underdeveloped state of infrastructure nationwide, and of the profound errors in thought about infrastructure that have allowed the situation to come about.

Treating the New York City transportation disaster as a local issue, or even a regional one, would be a grave

Dan Phiffer

New York City's overstretched subway system serves 5.5 million riders every weekday.

mistake. Trying to fix one problem at a time, and trying to finance projects on a local or regional basis, would be woefully insufficient, as the current state of affairs amply demonstrates. Instead, we should grasp this opportunity to upgrade our national economic thinking about infrastructure as a platform for higher levels of economic functioning and subsume New York City's needs in a broader context.

Here, we begin by posing answers to overlooked questions about the role of infrastructure in the economy. Equipped with those concepts, we approach U.S. national infrastructure needs in light of international infrastructure developments in China. Finally, we return to New York City, situated in its national and international context, and discuss the necessary next stages of its infrastructure development, looking not ten or twenty years into the future, but several generations ahead.

The Value of Infrastructure

It is not a surprise that the same economics profession that was oblivious to the coming collapse of the dot-com bubble, the 2007–2008 financial disaster, and the presently looming collapse of corporate debt, is hopelessly wrong about the value of infrastructure. Infrastructure projects are usually treated one at a time, and on a cost-benefit basis. Public-private partnership (PPP) financing is all the rage, with the expectation that private funds can be brought into infrastructure investment, in the hope that income generated by the completed project will be able to directly repay the investment. This approach to the economics of infrastructure is a total disaster, fundamentally failing to assess the true value of infrastructure.[1]

Rather than trying to build up an adequate understanding of infrastructure from components, it is best to begin afresh. To that end, consider infrastructure not as pieces and not only in the present, but as stages of successive platforms for human economic and scientific activity. First, view human history from the economic metric of *population* (rather than, say, GDP):

This change in the population of the human species over historical time reflects a unique characteristic of human beings as a species: the "carrying capacity" or "potential population density" of the human species is not fixed by nature—as it is for all other life—but is changed by the discoveries and practice of the human species itself. The source of this change in human population is our ability to discover principles of nature and of culture, and to implement those discoveries to form communities living at higher physical and cultural standards of living, better able to make the next level of discoveries in the future.

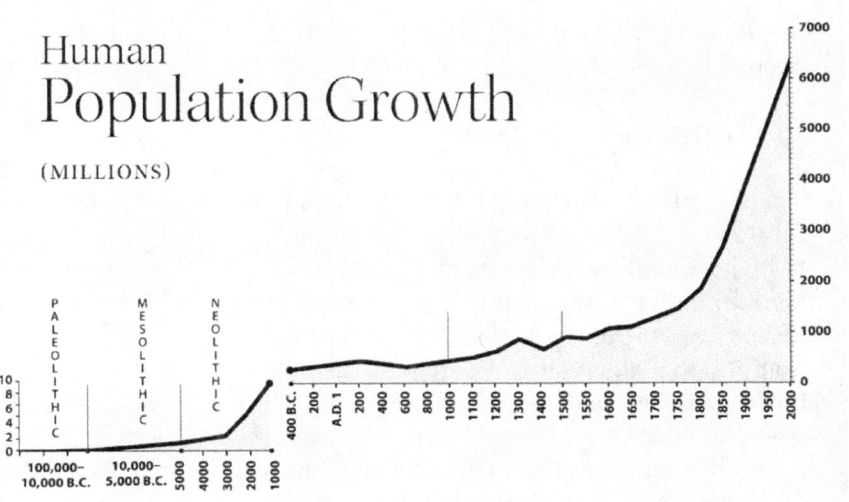

Human Population Growth

(MILLIONS)

Human population growth over time. If we were merely some type of less hairy ape, our population would never have exceeded a million or two. Not seen in this graphic is the increasing human population potential.

Concurrent with this mental and cultural development comes the transformation of the physical world itself. The importance of "natural" resources diminishes, as human civilization increasingly creates its own resources, liberating new potentials from materials and landscapes that were previously barren or inert—as in the cases of coal, petroleum, natural gas, metal ores, and uranium deposits. The importance of the "natural" state of the landscape fades, as irrigation brings blossoming life to deserts, as roads and canals bring cities and regions closer together, as telegraph wires carry thoughts nearly instantly, and as power lines transform the potential of the area they pass through.

In the words of the great American economist Lyndon LaRouche, writing in April 2010:

> We should then recognize that the development of basic economic infrastructure had always been a needed creation of what is required as a "habitable" development of a "synthetic," rather than a presumably "natural" environment for the enhancement, or even the possibility of human life and practice at some time in the existence of our human species.... Man as a creator in the likeness of the great Creator, is expressed by humanity's creation of the "artificial environments" we sometimes call "infrastructure," on which both the progress, and even the merely

---

1. Estimates of the U.S. infrastructure deficit range from a $2 trillion gap out of $4.5 trillion required over ten years (ASCE) to $8 trillion as assessed by head of the China Investment Corporation, Ding Xuedong.

continued existence of civilized society depends.[2]

And in September of that year:

The fact of the matter is, that the precondition for the rise of cultures to revolutionary changes to higher qualities of regions of sustainable, potential relative population-density, depends on virtual leaps in potential relative, human population-density which, in turn, require a higher quality of physical-cultural "platform" within which to operate... In other words, the level of achievable productivity depends upon raising the "platform," through revolutions in infrastructure, on which successful general advances in potential relative population-densities depend. Without those advances in basic economic infrastructure, merely particular technological progress locally applied will fail in attempted performance of the truly vital mission of physical-economic program, failing for lack of the progress in advancement of the quality of the infrastructural platform on which the success of the society as a whole depends.[3]

Considered on the long scale, we think of the platforms of ocean navigation by the stars and of coastal civilizations, of the development of irrigation and moves further inland, of canals and roadways, of the development of the rail transport made possible by the steam engine, of the electromagnetic revolution launched in the 1800s to 1900s, of the aborted potentials of the nuclear era, and of expanding our reach to space.

The *value* of the development of the steam engine and rail transport cannot be measured by adding up savings on freight charges, or the reduced expense of coal for steam engines compared to oats for horses. The value lies in the expanded potential of the human species as a whole, a value that is not captured by adding the components.[4]

2. *"What Your Accountant Never Understood: The Secret Economy"* EIR, April 17, 2010.
3. The Economic Past Is Now Behind Us! Money or Credit?
4. In an April 7 presentation at the New York University Tandon School of Engineering, I considered three specific failures of economists to comprehend the value of infrastructure: its incommensurable value, its

Rather than approaching infrastructure projects one at a time to determine whether they would bring back a "return on investment," we must consider our national needs as a whole.[5] In doing so, it is useful to first take a brief survey of the stunning achievements of Chinese infrastructure development in the last few decades.

China

China's explosive growth over the past several decades has brought 700 million people out of poverty and transformed a nation with among the lowest per capita GDP levels in the world, to be an international leader in an expanding array of advanced fields. What lessons can be learned from China's rise, particularly from its transportation infrastructure growth?

China's expansion of its rail transportation network could not be more dramatic. In 1997, when China began to focus on upgrading and speeding up its rail network, the nation's railroads operated at an average speed of only 48 km/h (30 mph). Over ten years, new trainsets and rail upgrades brought the speeds of some lines up to 160 km/h and 200 km/h. In the last decade, China has gone from having no high-speed trains (defined as achieving at least 250 km/h), to being the world leader, with 22,000 km (14,000 mi) installed, more than all of the high-speed rail in the rest of the world combined.[6] This astonishing development of high-speed rail took less time than the typical decade-long planning and approval process for a new highway in the United States. By 2035, China plans to have an eight-by-eight, 45,000-km high-speed rail grid stretching across the nation. Due to the twin difficulties of right-of-way acquisition in developed areas and the need for track to be rela-

non-local effects, and the inherently indirect nature of the return on investment. See "The Economic Value of Infrastructure."
5. Consider the proposal to upgrade the Soo Locks at Sault Ste. Marie. Currently, only one of the locks, Poe Lock, is capable of allowing passage for large lake freighters between Lake Superior and the lower Great Lakes. A 2005 study on upgrading the lock system to have a second lock capable of handling these larger ships recommended against its construction, reasoning that the return on investment would only be 75 cents of benefit for each dollar spent. Yet, according to the Department of Homeland Security, the failure of Poe Lock would result in a loss of 11 million jobs!
6. For more on the lessons to be learned from China's rapid development, see Bob Ingraham's article in the June 2, 2017 EIR, "Don't 'Repair' the System: Join the Belt and Road Initiative."

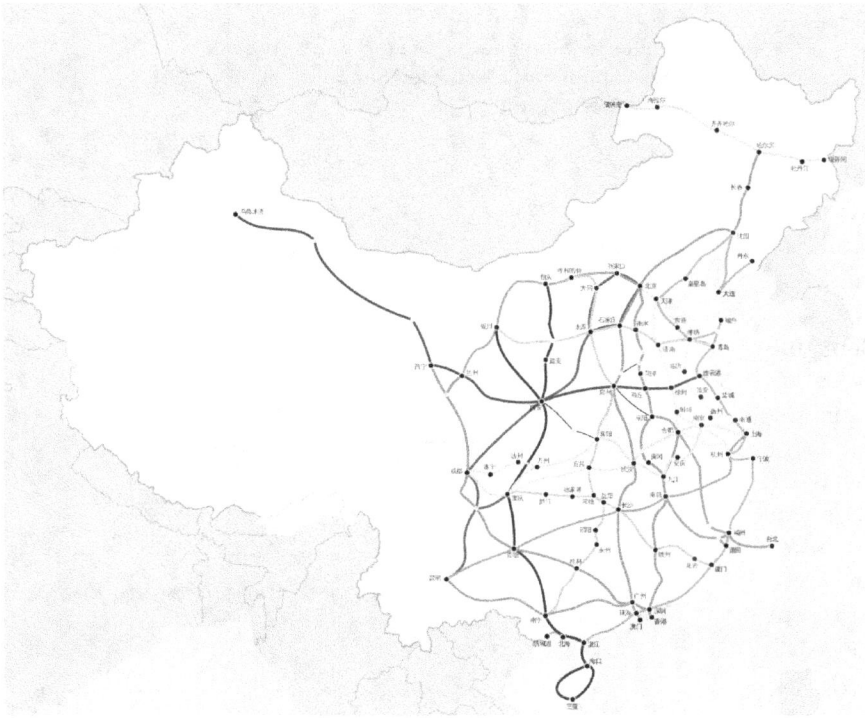

Li Chao

By 2035, China plans to have an advanced, top-of-the-line high-speed rail grid serving the nation.

km/h, was built in Shanghai, by the German firm Transrapid. The line opened for operation in 2004. Since then, China has developed its own domestic expertise in maglev construction, with a low-medium speed line currently operating in Changsha since 2016, and a maglev extension to the Beijing metro system slated to open later this year. As domestic technology further matures, it can be expected that China will be eager to export maglev trainsets.

Moving beyond transportation, consider another economic metric: energy use. Total per capita energy consumption in China has increased five-fold in the past quarter century. Even more dramatic than the overall increase in energy use has been the increase in electricity consumption per capita. Electrical power generally represents a higher capability to accomplish work than other forms of energy, and this value has increased an astonishing *25 times* over the same period. The availability of plentiful energy is an essential component of China's infrastructure platform.

tively straight to achieve high speeds, some of these lines lead to stations outside the most-developed downtown areas of the cities they serve. This provides an opportunity for new growth in these areas.

One stunning accomplishment was the completion of the Beijing-Shanghai High-Speed Railway, a 1,318-km (819-mi) high-speed railway that connects China's two largest cities. Construction began on April 18, 2008, and the line opened on June 30, 2011, just over three years later. Currently, the non-stop train from Beijing to Shanghai operates at an average speed of 300 km/h, and the trip takes less than five hours, compared to seventeen hours two decades ago.

Intra-city rail has also seen tremendous growth. In 1990, only Beijing, Tianjin, and Hong Kong had subway systems. By 2020, forty cities will have subway systems. At present, the top two subway systems in the world, measured in terms of ridership, are those of Shanghai and Beijing.

The next level of rail technology is magnetic levitation. Such trains leave behind the friction wheel-on-rail design altogether, instead being levitated and propelled by electromagnets. The world's first commercial maglev high-speed rail line, which runs at over 400

Wikipedia user BayCrest

The domestically engineered and manufactured maglev train in Changsha, China, has been in operation since 2016.

Exporting the Chinese Miracle

Perhaps most significantly, China is now acting to export this economic miracle via the Belt and Road Initiative. This proposal, launched by President Xi Jinping in September 2013, reflects decades of organizing work by Lyndon and Helga LaRouche and their collaborators. Through its own state institutions, and via new international financial institutions, such as the Asian Infrastructure Investment Bank, the Silk Road Economic Fund, and the New Development Bank, China has created the financing and technical potential for a tremendous boom of cross-national infrastructure and business development. Chinese state institutions have lent the equivalent of over $300 billion for infrastructure projects internationally since the Belt and Road Initiative began. Examples of recent international successes are the Addis Ababa-Djibouti Railway (completed in 2016), the Mombasa-Nairobi Standard Gauge Railway project (completed in 2017), and the new Karakoram highway and Gwadar Port (currently under construction in Pakistan).[7]

China stands poised to engage internationally on large infrastructure projects both through its developed technical and manufacturing expertise and base (particularly for rail and trainsets) and through its extensive financing abilities. For example, Ding Xuedong, the chairman of Chinese Investment Corporation, which holds tens of billions in U.S. Treasuries, announced in January that the fund would be eager to invest a portion in U.S. development projects.

Our National Needs

We must ask "what are the total infrastructure needs for the United States, in the increasingly interconnected world, as viewed several generations into the future?"[8] As we sketch out an answer to this question, there are

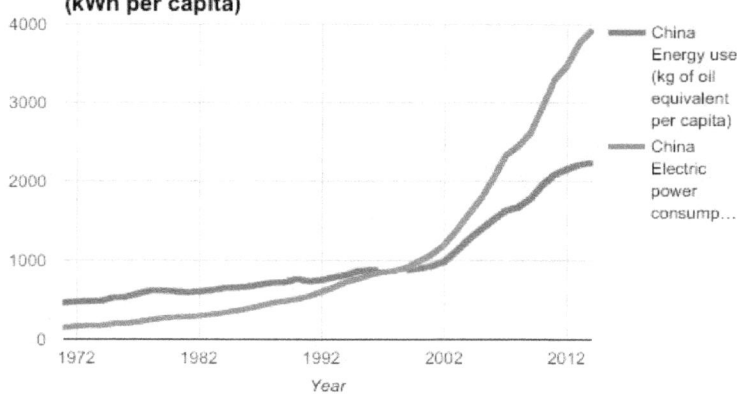

China: annual energy use (kg of oil equivalent per capita) and electric power consumption (kWh per capita)

— China Energy use (kg of oil equivalent per capita)
— China Electric power consump...

World Bank

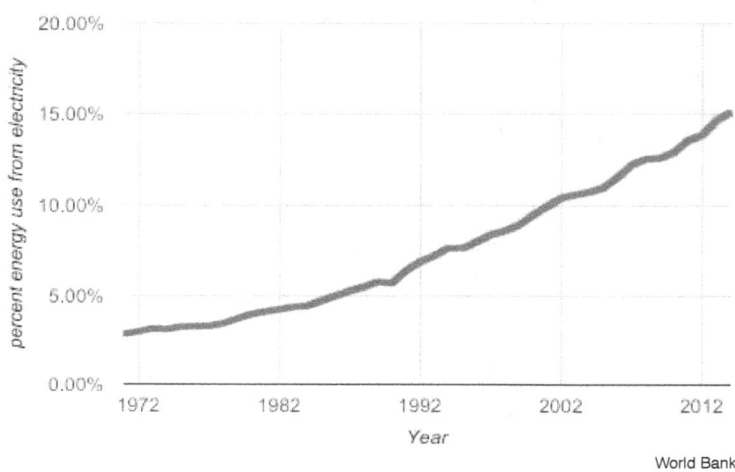

China: electricity as percentage of energy use

World Bank

several categories of infrastructure platforms to consider.

Power and Energy

Through most of U.S. history, power use increased on a per-capita basis, and the source of that power changed. Wood gave way to coal, preserving forests and bringing down the cost of providing power, and making steam engines possible. Coal lost its pre-eminence to fluid hydrocarbons. Nuclear technology, poised to become a major source of power, had an abortive growth. Its spread was sabotaged, preventing it from fulfilling its potential as a higher level of power.

In startling contrast to the overall rise in per-capita power use throughout our nation's earlier history, this

---

7. Thanks in large part to China-based financing, Africa is leading the world in its rate of new rail development.

8. We emphatically do *not* ask "What can the United States, on its own, afford at present?"

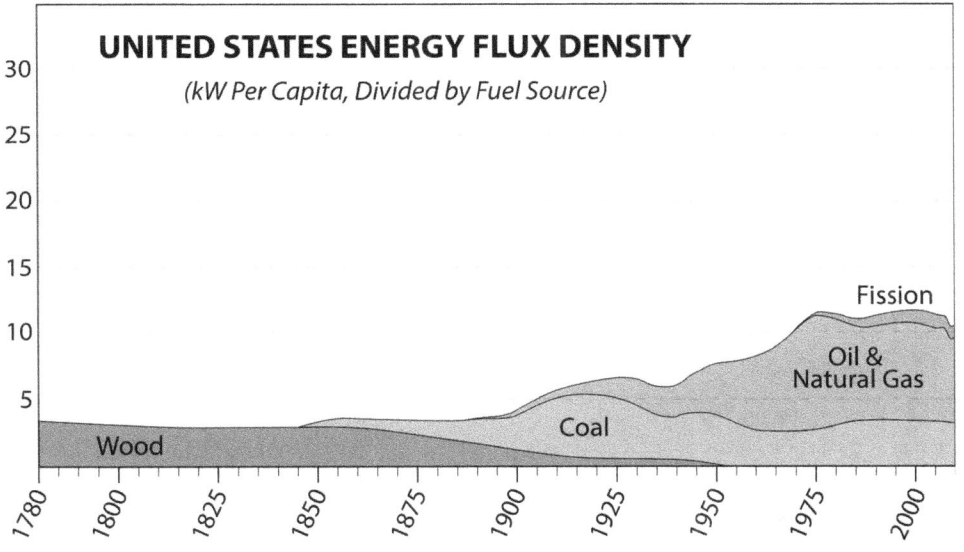

UNITED STATES ENERGY FLUX DENSITY
(kW Per Capita, Divided by Fuel Source)

The per-mass energy content of various energy sources. Wood, coal, and petroleum are burned to release their chemical energy. Uranium is made to undergo fission in a nuclear reactor to release nuclear energy, as does deuterium in the process of nuclear fusion. Anti-matter can be converted directly to energy as expressed by Einstein's famous relationship that $E = mc^2$.

value peaked in the 1960s,[9] and has stagnated since, reflecting the shift to a physically less productive economy.

When higher levels of power per capita and per square kilometer can be created at the same relative physical cost to society, the cost for existing applications is lowered, new processes with higher total power requirements become economical, and new physical reactions, associated with new domains of physical chemistry, become possible.

This was seen in the electrochemical revolution, whereby previously inaccessible or enormously expensive materials (such as aluminum) were made a common part of production, and the new principles of electromagnetism themselves replaced the simple motion of the steam engines they supplanted, as in today's computer-controlled machining, electron-beam welding, and electric discharge machining. Just as steam power freed mechanical production from dependence on geography (wind or running water), electricity allows production to be sited anywhere. And unlike steam engines, which require coal on-site to power them, electric

motors require only wiring to connect them to power plants.

The next level requires a crash effort for the full realization of the long-delayed nuclear economy, starting with mass production of cheaper and safer fourth-generation nuclear fission reactors (including the medium-term development of the thorium fuel cycle), and moving rapidly to the development of nuclear fusion. There is a fundamental limit to the capabilities of physical power sources (such as wind or hydro power) and chemical power sources (such as hydrocarbons). Nuclear forces are inherently five to six orders of magnitude greater than chemical forces, and will be the absolutely essential next stage of power development for the future of the human species. The development of controlled fusion will be the greatest of achievements, comparable to the creation of steam power.

Water

Water is the most ancient among the resources created by human beings, through the irrigation and dams of the ancient past, and through the future potential of large-scale water transfer, desalination, and weather modification projects. By adopting a continental-scale approach, with new technologies and scientific principles at our disposal, we can ensure the North American water cycle provides ample water for growing economic and biospheric needs.

Instead of hoping that rain will fall, we can mimic the cosmic-ray influences on cloud nucleation and improve the weather. Rather than looking forlornly out at the Pacific Ocean while lacking fresh water for human use, we can desalinate seawater. We need not look with powerless dismay at the imbalance of over-abundant water in the Northwest and droughts in the southwestern regions. The grand design of the North American Water and Power Alliance (NAWAPA) would divert

---

9. During which time the Eisenhower Interstate Highway System was taking shape, the Civil Rights movement was scoring major victories, and the nation was fulfilling Kennedy's goal of sending man to the moon.

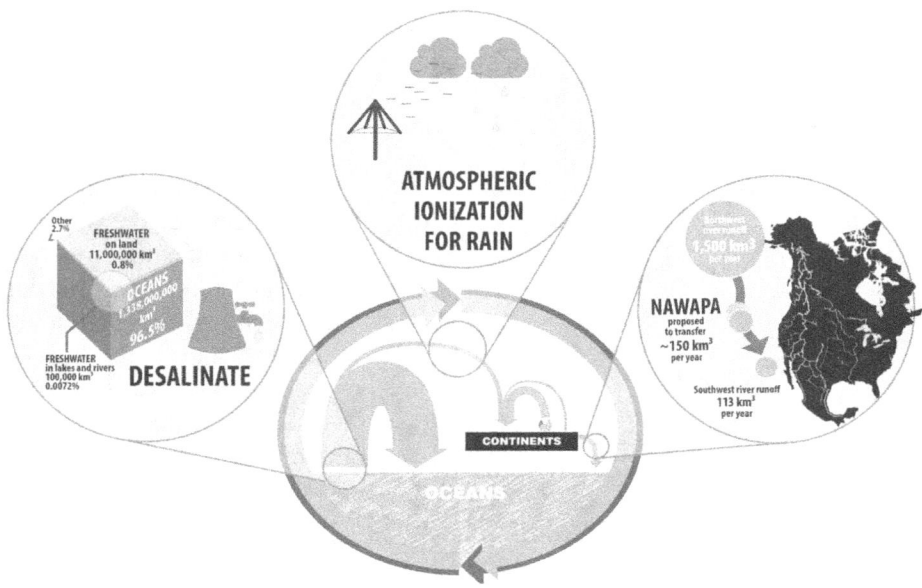

Technologies exist to intervene at all stages of the water cycle: desalinating seawater, causing rain by atmospheric ionization, and by rerouting water that has fallen as precipitation, as demonstrated by the proposed North American Water and Power Alliance.

5% to 10% of the abundant freshwater runoff where it is in excess, and transfer it to drier climes.

Existing water shortages and mounting water crises, typified by the conditions of California and the High Plains Ogallala Aquifer, will be overcome, and new territories will be opened for development.

Transportation

A modern high-speed and magnetic levitation rail system does more than increase speed and convenience of transportation: It changes the entire physical-economic space-time characteristics of the economic system. More extensive areas become accessible in less time, ensuring that more diverse population centers, manufacturing capabilities, and agricultural regions can all be economically accessible to the individual or productive process. The nineteenth-century construction of the railroads did much more than make shipping faster and cheaper: it allowed new types of production to occur, made otherwise useless resources viable, and sped the social interchange of ideas and people in the nation. Looking to the future, advanced systems of vacuum tube transport could provide supersonic access between selected regions.

In the full context of the proposed World Land-Bridge, the U.S. transportation network would be connected with other continents: with the Belt and Road Initiative in Asia via Canada and the Bering Strait connection that will link Russia and Alaska, and with Central and South America by building through the Darién Gap. The Bering Strait connection will not only allow the exploitation of the plentiful mineral and other Arctic resources, which are currently inaccessible; it will mean quicker freight transport between the continents, cutting in half the time taken for ocean-borne transportation. Closing the Darién Gap will, for the first time, allow land routes to connect the Americas as a whole. Considered in the context of the new canal across Nicaragua, currently under construction, and the bi-oceanic rail corridor passing through Bolivia as it stretches from Peru to

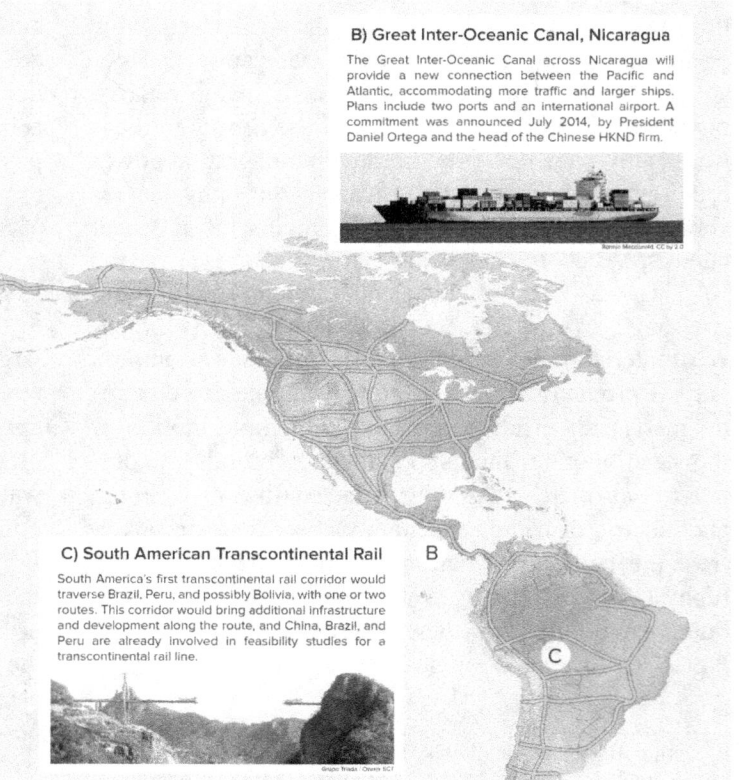

B) Great Inter-Oceanic Canal, Nicaragua

The Great Inter-Oceanic Canal across Nicaragua will provide a new connection between the Pacific and Atlantic, accommodating more traffic and larger ships. Plans include two ports and an international airport. A commitment was announced July 2014, by President Daniel Ortega and the head of the Chinese HKND firm.

C) South American Transcontinental Rail

South America's first transcontinental rail corridor would traverse Brazil, Peru, and possibly Bolivia, with one or two routes. This corridor would bring additional infrastructure and development along the route, and China, Brazil, and Peru are already involved in feasibility studies for a transcontinental rail line.

Examples of Inter-Oceanic and Transcontinental transportation modes in the Americas.

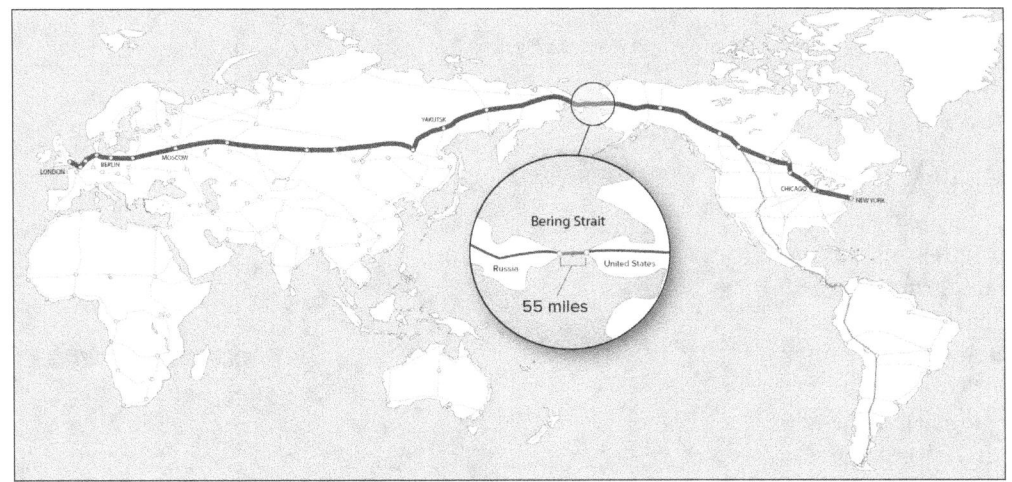

Via an inter-continental connection at the Bering Strait, the United States can directly join the Belt and Road Initiative. By closing the Central-South American Darién Gap, the Americas as a whole can be integrated.

week or two. As a simple matter of physics, the nuclear bonds of the atom are 100,000 to 1,000,000 times more energetic than the chemical bonds that hold together the molecules that are the basis of chemical fuels.

A century from now, powered by nuclear fission and fusion rockets, mankind's power over nearby space will include the ability to defend against threatening asteroids and comets, the opportunity of making use of resources on the moon and asteroids, and the dramatic potential of mining lunar helium-3 as the ideal fuel for nuclear fusion reactors back on Earth.

Brazil, the Darién connection can enable a dramatically upshifted level of connectivity and collaboration among the three Americas: North, Central, and South.

Space

Human infrastructure has extended beyond the confines of the Earth for millennia, in the form of astronomical navigation on the seas. In fact, life itself has developed extraterrestrial resource utilization in the form of the shift from the chemosynthesis of early life to photosynthesis, which provides the vast majority of energy for the biosphere today. With the advent of the space age in the mid-1900s, human space infrastructure has dramatically advanced. Satellites and probes provide us with navigation and imagery on the Earth, with knowledge of our heavenly neighbors and insights into the development of the Solar system, and with the expanding potential for further exploration and resource utilization. But we are running against a fundamental limit to our ability to expand our control over nearby space: the limits of chemical reactions.

The problem presents itself in the immense weight of chemical fuel relative to the travel and thrust of a rocket. A typical payload requires over 10 times its weight in fuel. While different space technologies, such as air-breathing first stages coupled with rockets, can improve this to some degree, there is an inherent limit in the potential energy in chemical bonds. Only by moving to nuclear fuels can a new level of space capabilities be reached. A nuclear-powered rocket could fire continuously on a journey to Mars, reducing the travel time from the better part of a year, down to a

A Return to New York

With these categories of infrastructure platforms in mind, return to New York City from a national, international, and extraterrestrial perspective. What will we wish to have done, a century from now, in New York? In 2117, while New York City will continue to play a unique role in the United States, entirely new cities will have been developed in the region, fostered by the new transportation network that will have been built, and the new productive capabilities unlocked by nuclear fusion. In this context, New York's connectivity with the broader region will be dramatically upgraded, and transportation within the city will be far more efficient.

We begin by assessing the current conditions, and then we will consider proposals for future development.

Current Conditions

First, some basics of the infrastructure.

New York's Metropolitan Transit Agency (MTA) subway system comprises 660 miles of customer track; 472 stations (more than any other system in the world), almost all operating 24 hours a day; and an additional 180 miles of other track (such as in rail yards). It currently provides nearly 1.8 billion rides annually, with ridership levels reaching new fifty-year highs.

The Long Island Rail Road (LIRR, owned by the MTA) comprises more than 700 miles of track and 124 stations. It averages one-third of a million passengers every weekday, with major stations at Penn Station, Atlantic Avenue, and Jamaica Station.

Metro-North Railroad (MNR) also comprises more than 700 miles of track and over 100 stations, with its major terminal at Grand Central Terminal, which has 44 platforms, more than any other rail station in the world.

New Jersey Transit (NJ Transit), with 540 track miles, runs an average of 700 trains every weekday. NJ Transit buses benefit from the exclusive bus lane at the Lincoln Tunnel, leading to the Port Authority Bus Terminal, which averages nearly a quarter-million passenger rides per day. On average, 1,850 buses per hour use the exclusive lane during peak commuting time on weekdays, totaling nearly 20 million passenger rides per year. This exclusive bus lane is at full capacity, as determined by the ability to move buses through the Port Authority Bus Terminal.

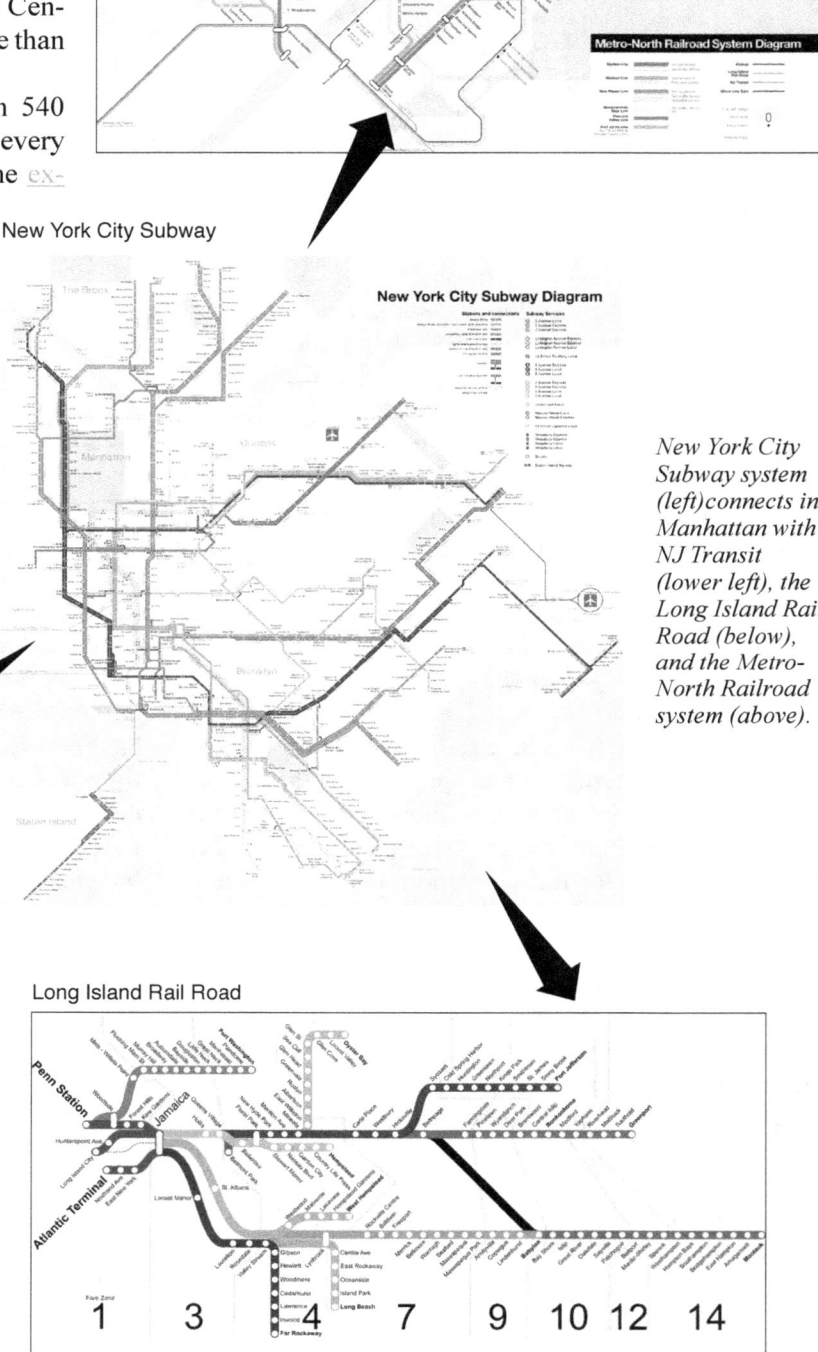

Metro-North Railroad System

New York City Subway

NJ Transit

Long Island Rail Road

New York City Subway system (left) connects in Manhattan with NJ Transit (lower left), the Long Island Rail Road (below), and the Metro-North Railroad system (above).

Pennsylvania Station, located between 31st and 33rd Streets and 7th and 8th Avenues, serves as a terminal for NJ Transit trains arriving via a dual tunnel under the Hudson River, as a terminal for Long Island Rail Road trains arriving via four tunnels under the East River, and as a station for Amtrak trains. During peak commuting times, Penn Station's 21 tracks service 20 NJ Transit trains, two dozen LIRR trains, and 4 Amtrak trains per hour. These levels are significantly higher than they were one or two decades ago, as more mass-transit commuters are added than car commuters every year. Overall, NJ Transit ridership into New York has tripled over the past three decades, and the growth is continuing. The infrastructure cannot handle these loads.

The Hudson tunnels and the East River tunnels are a century old and in desperate need of repair. This summer, two of the four East River tunnels will be closed for an estimated two months for necessary maintenance, while the only possible respite for the Hudson tunnels would be the building of entirely new Hudson tunnels, allowing the current ones to be closed for extensive maintenance. The major maintenance required on the L Train line, whose East River tunnels were flooded during Superstorm Sandy, will require closing that line for an estimated 15 months over 2019-2020.

Because of differences in power supply (different means of transmission—catenary versus third rail, and different third-rail configurations—and different voltages) and railcar height and width, it is not presently possible to fully inter-operate NJ Transit, LIRR, Amtrak, and Metro-North trains. For this reason, and due to differences among the operating agencies, Penn Station does not currently function as a through-station, which would allow LIRR trains to continue west to New Jersey and NJ Transit trains to continue east. This would require a standardization or double-powering approach, as well as adjustable platforms capable of accommodating different types of railcars. These separate rail lines could be consolidated under a broader regional network.

Two other Hudson crossings exist for the Port Authority Trans-Hudson (PATH) train system: one that crosses from Hoboken, NJ to Greenwich Village and then travels up 6th Avenue to 33rd Street, and one that crosses to Manhattan further south, providing service to the World Trade Center. At present, there is no underground mass-transit connection between the PATH station at 33rd, the MTA subway station at 34th St.-Herald Square, and Penn Station, one block further west.

A significant change to the region's transportation network, scheduled for completion in 2022, is the East Side Access project, the construction of a new tunnel under the East River at 63rd Street to connect the LIRR to additional tracks built below Grand Central Terminal. It is hoped that this would reduce the pressure on Penn Station from the LIRR.

The New York MTA subway system currently serves 5.5 million riders every workday, with the numbers sometimes swelling above 6 million per day. The subway system, relying in places on switch electronics that date back to the Franklin Roosevelt Administration, is an amazing engineering accomplishment of the past, but one that is presently operating far beyond its design capacity and is being pushed to beyond the breaking point. Over one-third of all train delays are due to overcrowding, which lengthens station dwell times and reduces system throughput.

Trains move slowly: Following a 1995 deadly train collision on the Williamsburg Bridge, the entire system has been running at reduced speeds, now averaging only 17 miles per hour. Besides the upgraded L and 7 trains, the entire subway network uses the outdated block-signaling approach for train distancing. The more modern technology, communication-based train control (CBTC), could enable safe operation of trains at closer distances, increasing capacity by up to 15%.

The open nature of the platforms presents additional difficulties. Trash discarded onto the tracks leads to track fires that cause hundreds of delays every year. Similarly, the lack of platform doors between the platform and the tracks makes it difficult to effectively air-condition the stations or to provide safety against falling onto the tracks.

Rail transport from New Jersey to the eastern part of New York is extremely limited. Railcars must either go north and cross the Hudson at Albany, adding nearly 300 miles to the journey, or use the New York New Jersey Rail (NYNJR) float barge, which transports up to 14 railcars each way on its two daily round trips from Jersey City to Brooklyn's 65th Street Rail Yard. This extremely low capacity means that most goods are instead transported by truck. Plans for a rail freight tunnel from New Jersey directly to Brooklyn date back decades.

So much for the present state of affairs of the New York transportation grid. Let's consider proposed improvements.

New York's Future

It must be said outright that it is impossible to satisfy future needs by "fixing" New York's system; the

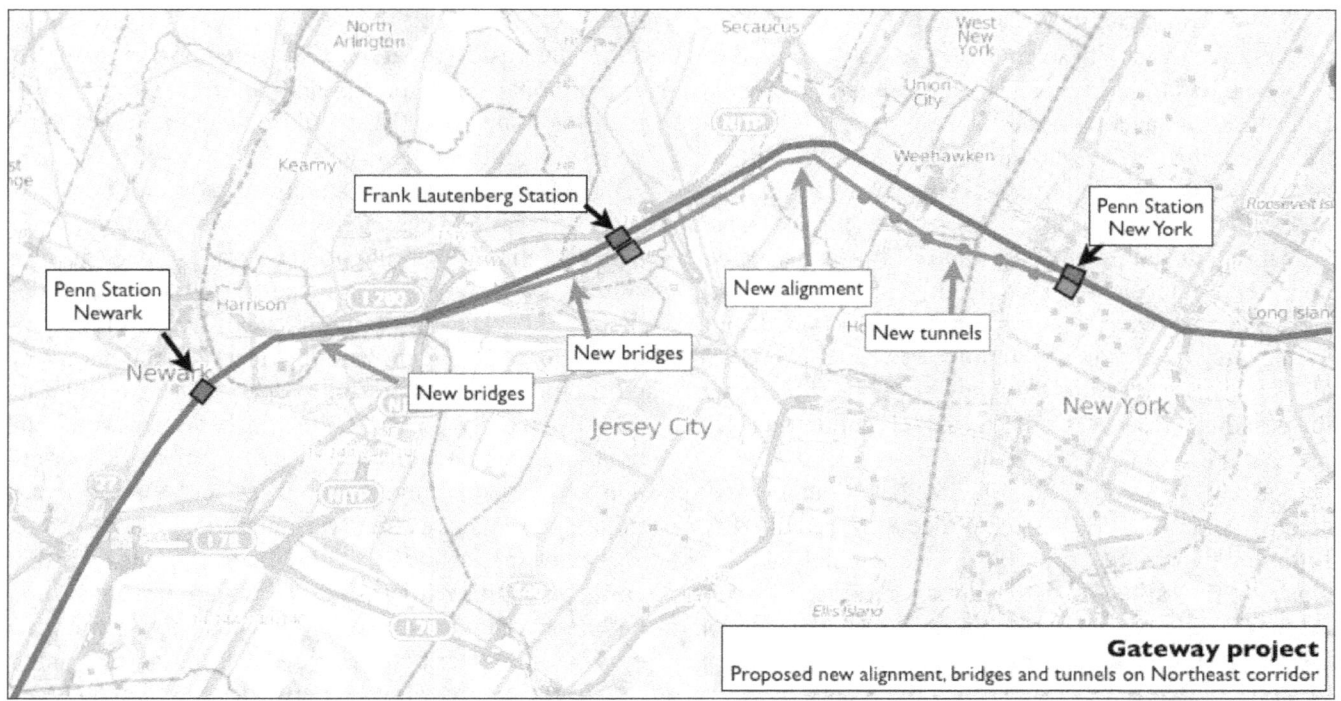

Amtrak's proposed Gateway Project, which would bring extra rail lines from Newark Penn Station and a Secaucus Loop to Manhattan's Penn Station.

system must instead be re-envisioned from a higher standpoint. In doing so, it is useful to have a sense of the many specific proposals for improvements, proposals made by numerous government agencies and officials, as well as planning and advocacy groups in the New York area. To get a sense of the already ongoing discussion, several of these proposals are discussed here, before we step back to take a larger view of the region from the standpoint of several generations in the future.

Some of the proposals are common-sense upgrades:

• Replace the entire signaling and switching system to the safer and more efficient CBTC technology, discussed earlier. The CBTC upgrade will also require replacing older railcars that are unable to be upgraded to interoperate with it (those purchased before 2000).

• Installing platform screen doors will increase safety, prevent track fires, and shorten train dwell times in stations, increasing throughput. Where space is available for installation of ventilation systems, these also allow for more efficient and effective climate-control of stations.

• At present, only one-fifth of the system's stations meet the accessibility standards of the Americans with Disabilities Act (ADA). While some would be very difficult to retrofit, it is possible to increase this proportion.

• Upgrading and standardizing the electrical sys-

tems of the commuter rail and Amtrak lines will make interoperation possible, and will eliminate the need for Amtrak to maintain dual-system trains (operating on both diesel and electric) for the Empire Line.

The urgent need to increase capacity for trans-Hudson commuters has been addressed in a variety of proposals:

• It has been proposed for years to build two new tunnels to connect to an expanded Penn Station. This is part of the plans of Access to the Region's Core (ARC, construction commenced in 2009, cancelled by New Jersey Governor Chris Christie in 2010), the Amtrak Gateway Project, and proposals by the Regional Plan Association, among many others. This would also involve adding a new connector at Secaucus Junction in New Jersey, to allow passengers to travel directly into New York without having to transfer as they presently must.

• Also proposed is the construction of four tunnels from Hoboken to an entirely new rail terminal in Manhattan on newly in-filled land at 14th Street, connecting to extended L and 7 trains.

• The efficiency of Penn Station can be increased by through-running, and creating new railyards for storage of trains prepared for the commuter rush in the opposite direction in the evening. This could be expanded into a broader regional upgrade with the build-

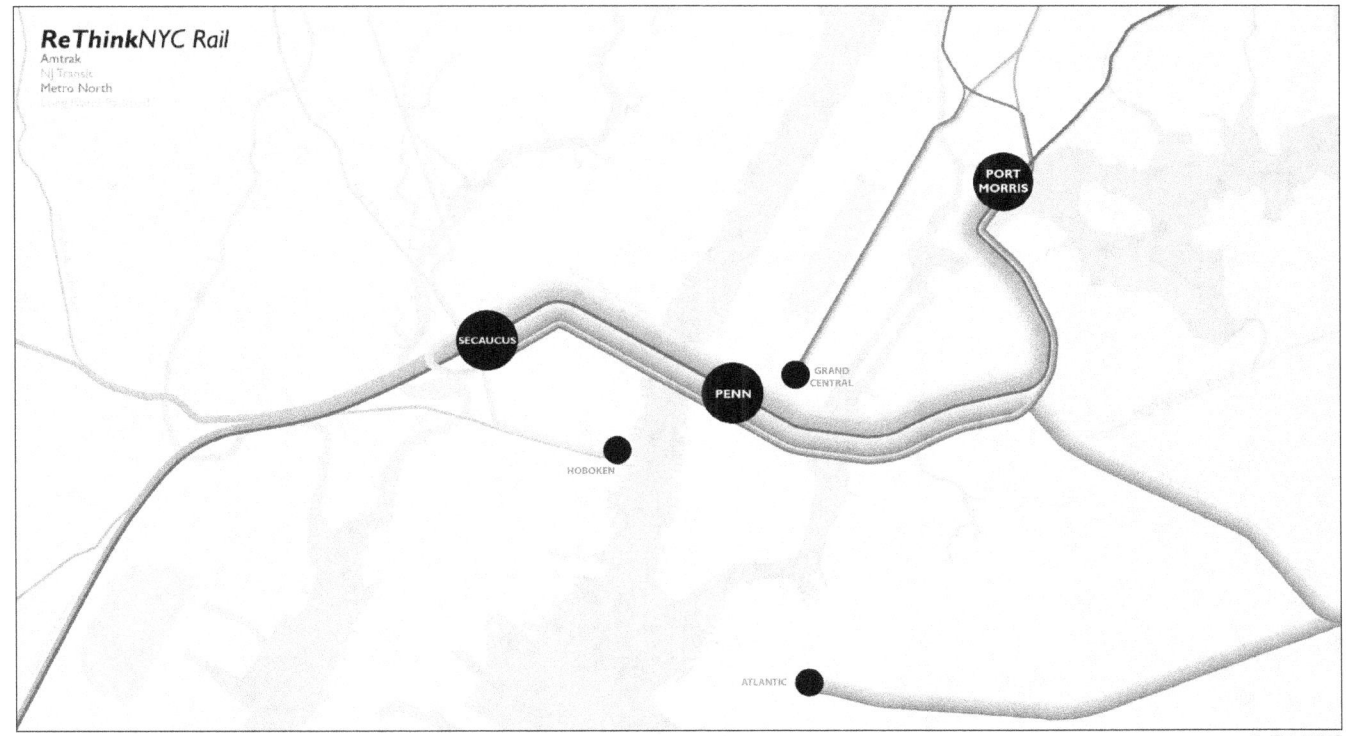

ReThinkNYC's proposal for how a through-running Penn Station would fit into the City's broader infrastructure network.

ing of expanded and entirely new rail hubs and yards in New Jersey, Queens, and the Bronx, as envisioned by ReThink NYC.

• The 2nd Avenue line, currently slated to reach Harlem, could be extended to the Bronx, as has been proposed since the 1960s, relieving the far-beyond-capacity 4, 5, and 6 lines.

• The region can move beyond the Manhattan-centered approach by building an entirely new Triboro MTA line, connecting the Bronx, Queens, and Brooklyn, as well as providing a denser grid of new lines throughout the City.

Regarding movement of goods, the need for east-of-Hudson freight rail access, which could dramatically reduce the vehicle-miles of truck traffic in the region (by over 100,000 truck-miles per day), has been addressed in proposals by the Cross Harbor Freight Program.

The Cooper Proposal

Dr. Hal Cooper is a rail transportation expert who has developed engineering pro-

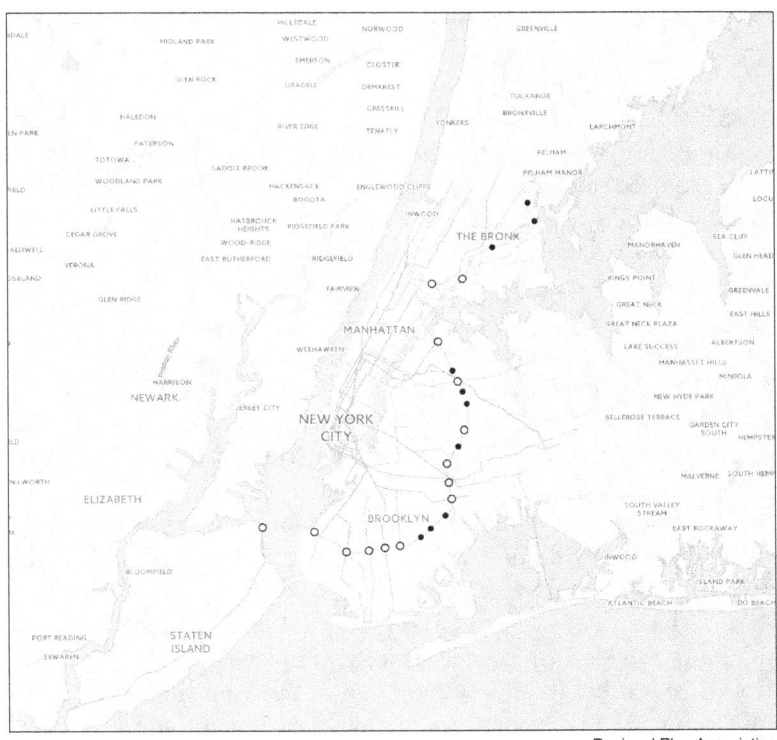

Recognizing the need to move beyond Manhattan-centered transportation, the Regional Plan Association has proposed a new Triboro subway line.

MTAβ

New York City's Hudson Yards, where the two tunnels from New Jersey enter Manhattan.

posals for, and lectured extensively on large-scale connectivity projects, such as the Bering Strait crossing with required rail connections in the Arctic, and bridging the Darién Gap to connect the Americas. He has served as a key catalyst in the development of the World Land-Bridge. Asked for his input, he has made the following proposals:

1. Build an underground rail connection from 37th Street to 32th Street between the Grand Central Terminal southern spur track in a north-south direction to the east-west main rail line under 32nd Street from the east end of Penn Station to the East River rail tunnel, to provide a direct rail connection between Penn Station and Grand Central Terminal for intercity passenger trains (Amtrak) and local commuter trains (LIRR, MNR, NJ Transit).

2. Make an above-ground rail connection from the rail line on the east end of the East River railroad tunnel from 32nd Street to the southern end of the Sunnyside railroad yard in Queens, to the western end of the Newton Branch rail commuter line of the LIRR, to connect LIRR and Amtrak.

3. Complete the conversion of the Farley Post Office to the west of Penn Station to make it the Amtrak rail passenger terminal, while Penn Station will continue to serve as a commuter rail station for NJ Transit and the LIRR.[10]

4. Build the new Alternative Rail Tunnel (ART) from New Jersey to the north and west of the existing Farley Post Office and Penn Station as previously proposed, to provide four-track rail tunnel access from New Jersey to Penn Station in Manhattan, immediately parallel to the existing two-track tunnel.

5. Then completely refurbish and replace the existing two-track rail tunnel from Secaucus in New Jersey to the west end of Penn Station.

6. Connect the existing PATH commuter rail transit line from Newark, New Jersey's Penn Station to the Newark Airport on the west, to the southern PATH line

---

10. Currently, the three rail lines using Penn Station (Amtrak, NJ Transit, and LIRR) each have their own concourses, ticketing, and waiting areas, all jammed in the same station.

to the World Trade Center in lower Manhattan, and then to the east to the Brooklyn Borough Hall and the Atlantic Avenue LIRR/subway station, so that a rail connection is possible between Newark and JFK airports.

7. As suggested by New York Governor Andrew Cuomo, build a rail connection (AirTrain) from LaGuardia Airport to the Mets-Willets Point Subway Station, potentially extending the connection all the way to the JFK AirTrain at Jamaica Station, providing a direct link between these two airports.

8. Build the subway connector from Bay Ridge, 95th Street, in Brooklyn under the Verrazano Narrows to connect with the existing Staten Island Rapid Transit (SIRT) rail link to a new Fox Hills station on Staten Island.

9. Construct a new freight railroad tunnel under the Lower New York Harbor, between the Greenville Yard in Bayonne, New Jersey, and the Fort Hamilton freight rail spur along the Bay Ridge railroad line through Brooklyn, to connect with the LIRR to transport trucks and other freight to a major intermodal terminal in Brooklyn or Queens.[11]

10. Expand the West Side rail line from the Henry Hudson Bridge in Upper Manhattan to Penn Station in Midtown for direct commuter and intercity railroad passenger service from Upstate New York.

11. Provide loop tracks or passenger train service centers at Secaucus in New Jersey, Woodlawn in the Bronx (MNR), and at Sunnyside Yard in Queens (LIRR).

12. Rebuild and refurbish the MTA subway signaling and communications systems and electrification/third-rail system infrastructure.

Dr. Cooper's proposals will be elaborated in a future article.

A Broader View

With the currently existing infrastructure and current upgrade proposals on the table, think of New York from the broader national and international context. The population of the United States is now around 320 million. What will it be in one hundred years? The New

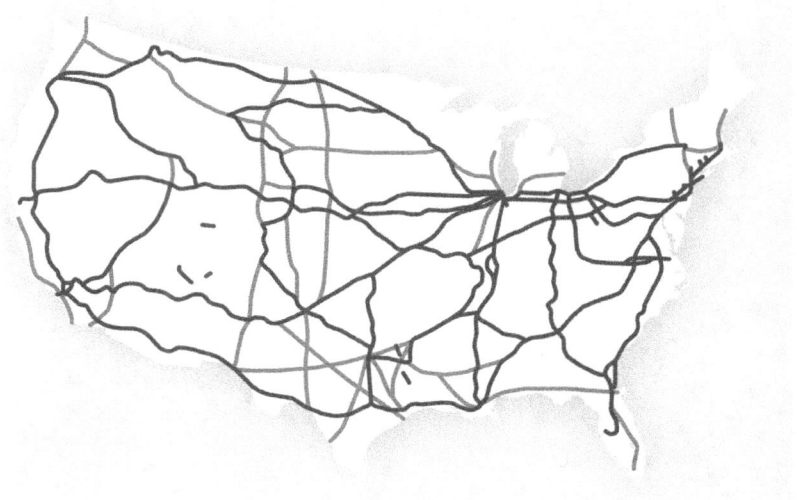

Cooper Consulting, *EIR*

Plans for an upgraded national rail network, including high-speed rail.

York Metropolitan region has over 20 million inhabitants. How many will live in the area in a century? The world's population presently stands at 7.5 billion. What will it be four generations from now? The path to the future does not lie in cleaning up and improving a transportation network that was built for a smaller population and a lower level of technology. To try to extend the present into the future is absolute incompetence. Start, rather, from a new, better future.

Resist the temptation to think of future New Jersey, Westchester, or Connecticut commuters reaching Manhattan in order to engage in occupations typical of the present. Instead, imagine travelers from Shanghai coming to New York by rail, stopping along the way to enjoy the Asian and American sides of the Arctic, as well as Chicago and the Great Lakes. Witness a railcar containing precision-manufactured optical components whizz by, as it travels from Brooklyn to Boise, Idaho for use in a new national laboratory there. Experience an integrated region as a whole, whereby the social, cultural, and educational opportunities for residents are dramatically increased by the ease of reaching multiple urban centers. Picture efficient rail lines carrying travelers on all routes less than several hundred miles, at which point accessible airports would be used. See the new cities developed by the confluence of new transportation, energy, and water corridors, their growth based on an upgradable, sustainable network of infrastructure.

In this future, the newly great New York City serves as a major hub, served by a nationwide high-speed or maglev rail network. The new lines built between New

_____
11. Consult the map of the "Cross-Harbor Rail Tunnel."

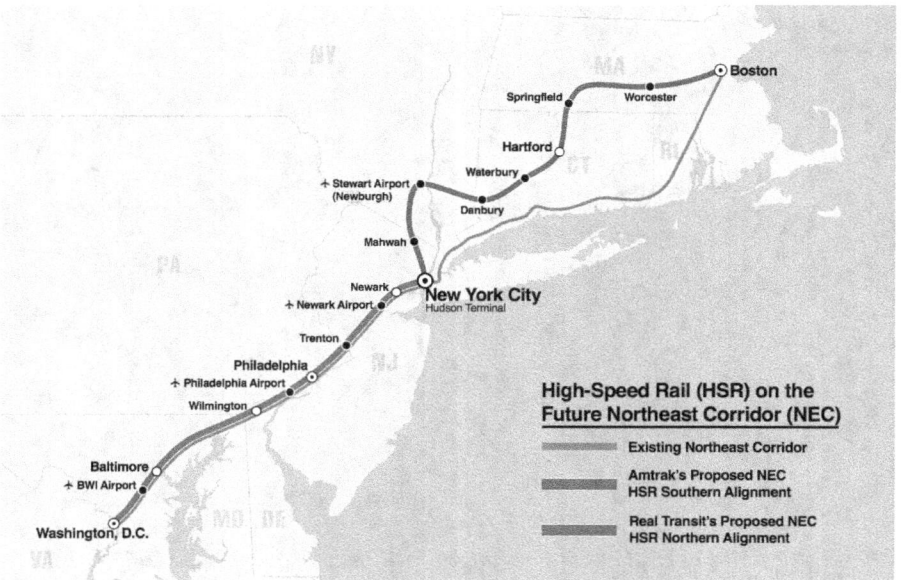

Real Transit, "Planning for a New Northeast Corridor," October 2014

High-Speed Rail (HSR) on the Future Northeast Corridor (NEC)

- Existing Northeast Corridor
- Amtrak's Proposed NEC HSR Southern Alignment
- Real Transit's Proposed NEC HSR Northern Alignment

RealTransit's proposal for a new, high-speed Northeast Corridor would abandon the current right-of-way north of New York City, adopting a new route to allow for straighter, faster tracks and service to areas neglected by current rail.

York and Boston, bypassing the old Northeast Corridor, bring new areas into prominence, and serve as a backbone for the next generation of development. Air travel is a breeze, with rail reducing demand on the City's three main airports, and with the expanded Stewart International Airport in Newburgh, NY (owned by the Port Authority of New York and New Jersey), less than half an hour from Manhattan by smooth and comfortable maglev rail. Future connectivity must be a process of leapfrogging.

While the specifics of future infrastructure are beyond the scope of this report, some principles of infrastructure development can be stated:

- New infrastructure platforms will be built in a way that can have the greatest impact for the future. This may mean building hubs, new universities, and high-speed connectivity in areas that are not currently densely populated. The infrastructure of the future, while planned with today's situation in mind, must emphatically be *for the future.*

- The most productive and densely utilized areas of today may not be the most important areas in the future. For example, the emphasis on connectivity to Midtown Manhattan exists today *because of past investments* in the area. It is Midtown's relatively excellent connectivity to the surrounding areas that has brought about its significant growth relative to the area between it and Downtown Manhattan. New infrastructure will make new centers, and this process should not be avoided! In the past, the location and spacing of cities were determined by both the natural and synthetic environment, by natural geography and by improvements in it, as well as transportation technologies. As we create a new platform of a synthetic, nurturing environment suited to our future needs, we will create new locations for development and entirely new cities.

- A process of leapfrogging must be the goal. While unsafe conditions should be repaired, the true vision of a national infrastructure renaissance must be setting the conditions for a qualitatively higher level of productivity for the future. Efficient movement of goods and people in urban centers oriented around productive employment, provided with plentiful and reliable energy and water—this is what is required.

- Higher technologies must be employed. For example, maglev transport is fundamentally superior to wheel-on-rail trains, and should be promoted both for its direct economic benefit, as well as to further research on the underlying technology.

- Government agencies and authorities capable of effective regional planning are required. For example, consider China's plans for the integration of the 100 million-person "Jingjinji" area, linking Bei*jing*, Tian*jin*, and parts of Hebei province (*Ji*). Through rail and roadway connections, and improved connectivity, this entire area will function as a single unit from a broad infrastructure standpoint.

- We require an active improvement in the productivity of the land. Bringing water, power, and transportation to isolated, parched, or otherwise impoverished areas instantly increases the relative potential of the area, making possible further investments in productive ventures and social life.

- Currently dilapidated and unsafe conditions requiring urgent repairs must be addressed. This includes such structures as dams, locks, bridges, levees, tunnels, and any other vulnerable infrastructure whose failure

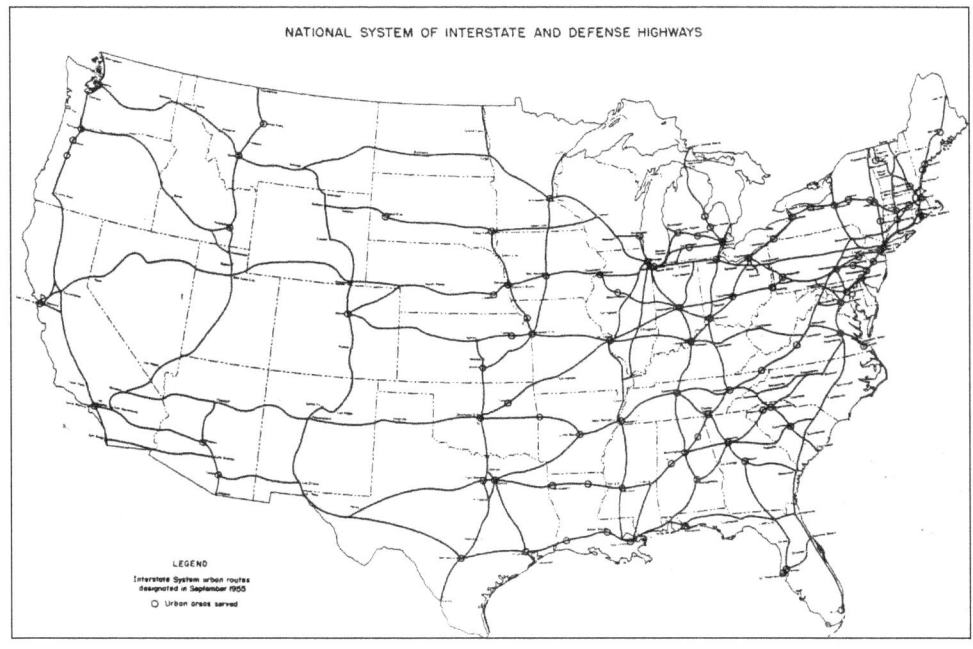

NATIONAL SYSTEM OF INTERSTATE AND DEFENSE HIGHWAYS

LEGEND
Interstate System urban routes
designated in September 1955
○ Urban areas served

The Interstate Highway System, as planned in 1955. In 1956, President Eisenhower separated this capital investment from the annual appropriation process, by setting up a special trust fund with a dedicated funding stream.

would have devastating effects.

• International cooperation is essential. At present, Chinese engineering, manufacturing, and financing all play a major role in infrastructure around the world. The United States stands to benefit greatly from U.S.-Chinese cooperation on such projects.

• Projects must be built with their future sustainability in mind.[12]

• A higher platform of national infrastructure must meet the needs of scientific research and of space exploration and settlement.

The best proposals from national, regional, and local perspectives can be developed anew by empowered and energized planning bodies able to count on sufficient credit.

Conclusions for Action

"How will we pay for all of this?" The simple truth is that current funding mechanisms will not work. If they were sufficient, New York, for example, would not be the transportation disaster it currently is. What is re-

quired is a national banking approach, whereby financing will not be through short-term appropriations, depending on annual legislative reapproval, but rather by longer term loans and through trust funds with dedicated, non-appropriations based funding. Unlike public-private partnerships, a national bank could properly reflect the indirect returns on such investments. Briefly, through specific taxes (such as an increased gasoline tax) or other revenue streams (in addition to user fees), such a national bank could capture the indirect benefits of infrastructure upgrades and finance long-term projects at reasonable interest rates.

In contrast, the attempt to treat the problem locally, in the context of a collapsing economy, has led to the situation where debt service is nearly as large as the entirety of the New Jersey Transportation Trust Fund's $1.2 billion incoming funds every year, and the MTA is $35 billion in debt. The long-term nature of the projects, and the non-localized, indirect nature of the benefits, demand appropriate means of financing. A national banking approach serves this function.

China's spectacular infrastructure success, fueled by government credit and credit guarantees, shows what can be done, and at what speed it can be accomplished, when there is a national mobilization for its achievement and a financial system that allows credit to flow to productive investments. In the United States, we desperately require the reinstatement of Glass-Steagall to stem the flow of funds into non-productive speculation, and a national credit program to invest in the future, in cooperation with international partners.

The call for $1 trillion in infrastructure investment over ten years, via public-private partnership financing mechanisms, will not work. A national *mission* is required—a mission for a more productive (and *happier*) United States, playing a positive role for the world's future. Under the right leadership, and with a healthy economic structure, the United States has much to offer the world!

---

12. See Richard Trifan's presentation on "Sustainability Needs of the New Silk Road Infrastructure" at an April 7 Schiller Institute–NYU Tandon School of Engineering event in Brooklyn.

Every Day Counts In Today's Showdown To Save Civilization

II. The Silk Road Dialogue

INTERVIEW WITH ZEPP-LAROUCHE

Belt & Road Initiative Instills Hope for Peace, Development Among Nations[1]

by Wan Lixin, *Shanghai Daily*

June 1—Helga Zepp-La-Rouche visited Shanghai for the first time in the summer of 1971. In 1977 she married American economist Lyndon LaRouche, and the couple have since worked together on development plans for a just, new world economic order.

Zepp-LaRouche founded the Schiller Institute in 1984, a think tank devoted to the realization of these plans and a renaissance and a dialogue of classical cultures.

In 1991 she was a coauthor of a study, *The Eurasian Landbridge/The New Silk Road*, and in 2014 of the study, *The New Silk Road Becomes the World Land-Bridge*, which has been translated into Chinese, Arabic, German, and Korean.

She is an expert in European humanist philosophy and poetry, Confucius, and history.

After attending the recent Belt and Road Forum in Beijing, she visited Shanghai, where *Shanghai Daily* reporter Wan Lixin interviewed her.

Wan: In what way do you think the Belt and Road Initiative is significant for the world and China?

Zepp-LaRouche: I think the Belt and Road Initiative signifies a revolutionary move to a new epoch of civilization. The idea of having win-win cooperation among nations is the first time that a concrete concept has been offered to overcome geopolitics.

Since geopolitics was the cause of the two world wars, I think it is a completely new paradigm of thinking, in which an idea proposed by one country has the national interest basically in coherence with the interests of humanity as a whole. This has never happened.

This has instilled tremendous hope among developing nations that they have the chance to overcome poverty and underdevelopment. And I think this is an initiative that will grow until all the continents are connected through infrastructure and development.

1. *EIR* has edited the text without abridging it. *Shanghai Daily* is an English-language newspaper. The interview can be seen here.

Wan: What do you think are challenges confronting the world today?

Zepp-LaRouche: I think the biggest challenge is that the trans-Atlantic financial system is in jeopardy, because the G7 countries did nothing after the financial crisis of 2008 to remedy the root causes of this crisis. The danger today is that we are going to have another financial crisis much worse than that of 2008.

In this light I think the financial system associated with the Belt and Road Initiative—the Asian Infrastructure Investment Bank (AIIB) and similar institutions, which are focussed on investment in the real economy, are an anchor.

Hopefully the Western nations will rethink their orientation of high-risk speculation and eventually go back to the banking system represented by the AIIB.

U.S. President Trump announced that he will go back to the American economic system of Alexander Hamilton, and that's potentially the kind of reform that makes the United States fit to cooperate in this new financial system.

The second challenge is naturally terrorism. This requires international cooperation, and there I think the Belt and Road could offer a lasting solution by extending the initiative to Southwest Asia and building up the economy in that part of the world, which has been destroyed by wars based on lies.

Why does one have to solve the problem of terrorism militarily first? You have to have an economic perspective so that people in the regions have hope for the future. So I think ending terrorism would require the Belt and Road Initiative and the reconstruction of the Southwest Asia and Africa.

Wan: There has been an evolving perception about globalization. How do you think the Belt and Road Initiative is reshaping this perception?

Zepp-LaRouche: The old globalization really went entirely in one direction. First of all, it made the deregulation of the markets and high-risk speculation easy.

And this increased the gap between the rich and the poor in an intolerable way in many countries.

This mode of globalization is being rejected, as you can see by the Brexit and the rise of many right-wing

Heads of State and Heads of Government at the opening session of the Belt and Road Forum, May 14, 2017.

movements in Europe. So this model has clearly failed.

I think the new Silk Road—the win-win cooperation as proposed by China—has developed at incredible speed in the less than four years since President Xi proposed it.

This new model of globalization is based on the common good of all participating countries. This is the more attractive form of globalization and this is why so many countries have joined it.

Wan: What do you think are some of the factors that need to be considered when it comes to implementing the Belt and Road Initiative across different cultures?

Zepp-LaRouche: The Schiller Institute has organized hundreds of seminars and conferences on the New Silk Road for 26 years.

We have always made the point that for this New Silk Road to succeed in the tradition of the old Silk Road, which was also an exchange of ideas and cultures, not just products and technology, you have to combine economic cooperation with dialogue between cultures.

This dialogue must be on the highest level, so each culture has to present examples of its best, such as Confucianism, Italian renaissance, and the German classical period. Each must present the best works of its arts—in music and poetry, painting, and other forms of art.

Our experience is that when people come into contact for the first time with expressions of such high culture from another culture, they are surprised by their beauty.

And this beauty then opens the hearts and souls of the people.

This is the best medicine against chauvinism, xenophobia, and prejudice, and it opens the way for the love of other cultures.

It is in conformity with Confucian teaching that all activity must be combined with strengthening of love for mankind, because without that cultural component, the New Silk Road will not flourish.

Wan: What do you think such high-profile events, such as the recent summit, suggest about China's role in world affairs?

Zepp-LaRouche: It a great honor for me to participate in this Belt and Road Forum, and I was deeply impressed by the speech of President Xi Jinping. Among all participants I spoke with, there is a consensus that we are actively participating in the shaping of history.

All this means that China is right now leading the world in terms of providing the perspective for the future.

I think this has been recognized by many countries in Latin America, Africa, and Asia, and even some European countries are starting to recognize that it is in their best interests to ally with that initiative. So I think it has been made clear that China is the only country right now that offers a positive perspective to overcome the strategic bottleneck of our present times.

Wan: In the past, the quest for prosperity invariably led to competition, strife, or wars. Is this avoidable?

Zepp-LaRouche: Concerning the question of competition, strife and war, I think this must be replaced by joint development.

Here I would like to quote from Pope Paul VI, who said that "Development is the new name for peace."

Wan: How do you think the West is responding to the Belt and Road Initiative?

Zepp-LaRouche: The responses have been mixed, because you have those who want to stick to the old geopolitical thinking, to the status quo of their power, and to their understanding of their power position.

I think this is an outdated way of thinking.

Many think-tanks of the West are still publishing re-

Xinhua
China is leading the world, providing the perspective for the future. Shown, President Xi Jinping addressing the Belt and Road Forum.

ports along these lines. But there is a wind of change.

Many European countries have realized the potential of collaborating with the Belt and Road, including Greece, Serbia, Hungary, Slovenia, Czech Republic, Italy, Spain, Portugal, and Switzerland. So I think this tendency will increase.

Those countries which are more reserved—such as Germany—will have to change. But I think German industries, particularly the middle-sized companies, are absolutely in cooperation with China in the Belt and Road Initiative.

Wan: Say something about your experience in China.

Zepp-LaRouche: I was first in Shanghai 46 years ago in 1971, after traveling on a cargo ship. Although it was not the best time to be in China, it awakened my love for China.

The city has changed completely. Except for some buildings on the Bund, I couldn't find anything that I have in my memory. I can not think of any other countries on the planet that have seen such gigantic changes.

I think the Chinese people are much too modest. They should feel more confident about what they have accomplished. They have created the biggest miracle in the world, even bigger than the post-war German economic miracle. They should be very proud to be Chinese.

The decision by Moody's Investors Service to cut China's sovereign ratings is insane. In German we have a saying, that one should take a good look at oneself before making a stupid criticism of someone else.

A Musical Dialogue of Cultures In Houston

by Brian Lantz

We have always made the point that for this New Silk Road to succeed in the tradition of the old Silk Road—which was also an exchange of ideas and cultures, not just products and technology— you have to combine economic cooperation with dialogue between cultures. This dialogue must be on the highest level, so each culture has to present examples of its best, such as Confucianism, the Italian renaissance, and the German classical period. Each must present the best works of its arts—in music and poetry, painting, and other forms of art.

—Helga Zepp-LaRouche

May 19—On May 16, the day after the Belt and Road Forum closed in Beijing—with the participation of 28 heads of state and government, and Schiller Institute founder Helga Zepp-LaRouche—an extraordinary concert in Houston, Texas, demonstrated the potential for bringing the United States into the New Paradigm represented by the Belt and Road. Under the banner of "A Musical Dialogue of Cultures," more than 100 guests celebrated the successful conclusion of the Beijing Belt and Road Forum—or were introduced to it by members of the Houston Schiller Institute Community Chorus— in a musical journey that circled the globe.

The response was a mixture of delight and surprise, with thoughtful reflection. As one participant commented, "I'm trying to figure out this A=432 thing. I think music is really important; the problem in the country goes so much deeper. ..." The audience came from every walk of life, and every nation of origin found in Houston, and many were hearing music they had never heard before.

Schiller Institute/Dwight Jarrett

Houston Schiller Institute Community Chorus.

Left: The auudience at the Houston, Texas, Belt and Road cultural celebration.

Below: Arturo Domingo

Schiller Institute/Dwight Jarrett

Schiller Institute/Dwight Jarrett

This concert represents a new stage in a pattern of growth, as well as recognition, of the Schiller Institute's role in organizing the residents of Houston, the fourth largest city in the United States, to open up to the world, learning about China's Belt and Road Initiative, and joining the Schiller Institute's efforts to cause the United States to become a partner in transforming this great endeavor into a true World Land-Bridge. To this end, there had been a coordinated outreach effort by members and activists, including distribution of fliers at events, campuses, workplaces, and online postings.

The community center which sponsored the event, also organized to build attendance. All of the musicians—who volunteered their time and efforts—invited friends and family. For example, Arturo Domingo, a Mexican-American tenor who performed two arias, had e-mailed out invitations, and brought a dozen guests—members of an international chorus that he sings with. Others posted colorful announcements on their Facebook pages, and otherwise helped build attendance. All these musicians are wrestling, in various ways, with the ideas of Lyndon and Helga LaRouche, the Schiller Institute, and the new Belt and Road/World Land-Bridge paradigm.

The Power of Music

Brian Lantz, who served as the Schiller Institute's Master of Ceremonies, began by briefly defining the inspiration for the concert: the Belt and Road Initiative, the success of the Belt and Road Forum in Beijing, and its global scope—in contradistinction to the horror stories dominating the U.S. media. There is actually reason for great optimism, Lantz stressed—nations and cultures can communicate. They can do so because they produce scientists and artists who believe in universal principles, which are actually true everywhere. The common ground of such principles, and the recognition of a higher principle of principles, create the basis for real dialogue. (There were affirmative murmurs and "Amens" in response.) This is the true basis for peace, through the development of all mankind. Throughout the evening, Lantz introduced the musicians and wove the various musical contributions together, as a kind of travel guide to the music, which circled the globe, nation by nation, throughout the ages.

The Houston Schiller Institute Community Chorus opened the program with "The Star Spangled Banner," followed by Mozart's "Ave Verum Corpus" and his "Bundeslied," a masonic piece pledging brotherhood to God and your fellow man, north and south, east and west. (All selections were preceded by short introductions, which included words from the musicians explaining them.) Tenor Arturo Domingo followed with a well-placed, ringing performance of "Jurame," by Maria Grever, to much delight. Two Indian-Americans, M.G. Shetty and Mrs. Sangeeta Panse, both ambassadors of classical Indian music in Houston, then performed two classical Indian compositions—the "Ragg Yaman," followed by a short Dhum of Indian folk melodies, both on Tabla and Sitar, further "stretching" and intriguing the responsive audience. Dorceal Duckens, bass-baritone, followed with a profound performance of "Dormiro Sol" from Verdi's opera *Don Carlos*. Duckens, also the maestro of the Community Chorus, brought real gravitas to the event throughout. Violinist Xia Xia Zhang, a noted soloist who has performed with us twice before, followed Mr. Duckens, which was perfect. She gave a skilled and impassioned performance of the Adagio and Fuga movements of J.S. Bach's Violin Sonata No. 1 in G minor. (One guest exclaimed afterwards that he had to look around a corner to see if Xia Xia was not playing *two* violins!) All of these performances drew great applause from an animated audience.

Schiller Institute /Dwight Jarrett
Mrs. Sangeeta Panse

The second half of the program opened with Arturo Domingo giving an operatic treatment to another Mexican composition, "Dime que si," riveting attention of the gathering. With his own "cheering section" of friends, he further livened up the on-going interaction of musicians and audience. Domingo was followed with an introduction to the traditional music of China, by Sylvia Yan, Francine Di, and Amanda Cheung, members of the ensemble Eastern Echo. They performed—on Dizi, keyboard, and Pipa respectively—the well known "Molihua" (Jasmine Flower) and "Song Ni Yi Zhi Meigui Hua" (Send Me a Rose), an intriguing folk song from Xinjiang province (Xinjiang Uyghur Autonomous Region) with a real Silk Road feel. It featured the Pipa, a popular, plucked instrument which has been played for almost two thousand years in China. The keyboard-playing introduced a western aspect which was somewhat distracting in the first song, but the audience was delighted all the same, particu-

Schiller Institute/Dwight Jarrett
Dorceal Duckens

larly by "Send Me a Rose," and by the deep participation of these three talented Chinese-American musicians in the evening's musical dialogue. Dorceal Duckens then followed, with "Didn't My Lord Deliver Daniel?" arranged by the great African-American composer Harry Burleigh. Dorceal again established a real moral high ground with a beautiful and powerful performance. He then brought the Schiller Community Chorus back to the stage and led them in two Spirituals, "I've been 'Buked," and "Deep River." Then followed another spiritual, the chorus of Hebrew slaves, "Va Pensiero," from Verdi's opera *Nabucco*, which awed the audience into hushed participation. "The Lord Bless You and Keep You," which Sylvia Olden Lee might consider a "white spiritual," closed out the program, with a diverse group of audience members quietly singing along to themselves.

Beauty that Moves the Soul

Part of what made the concert so successful was the wide variety of "hyphenated Americans" who came, and brought friends and their spirit. There was a

Xia Xia Zhang
Schiller Institute/Dwight Jarrett

great range of responses and comment. One young man in his 30s exclaimed, "This was just amazing! You know, all these different cultures are really talking about the same thing. . . . I see why this is so important right now." An Iranian salesman, who almost didn't come, was profusely grateful. There were Malaysian-Americans, Indian-Americans, African-Americans, Irish-Americans, and other groups. A Chinese-American lady, from the community center, brought a friend, and was very happy—it just showed. Other groups from the community center also came: members from a Bible study group and a "Point-Counterpoint" discussion group. A small businessman drove four hours (each way) just to come to the event, despite having come upon hard times just now, telling us afterwards, "I'm not good at adjectives. It was real good." An Egyptian-American (who is currently unemployed), said, "I just can't believe the quality of the singing. I didn't think I would come across this. . . ." One friend commented that he enjoyed the chorus best. It reminded me of when I was young, he said—as if that said it all. A young profes-

sional, who works on NASA-related programs, was totally happy and appreciative. She responded to a last minute call and brought a friend. A former youth activist was singing along with one of Arturo's Mexican pieces—he was so happy that Mexico was part of the program. A Bernie Sanders supporter, who knows us from various events, and was still put off by the slanders against LaRouche, loved it all. Challenged afterwards as to what he now thought about LaRouche, he quipped, "Oh, I'm coming around." He later e-mailed in his thanks: "I really enjoyed it. I'm looking forward to your next event." In sum, the audience was moved by the overlap of beautiful music, personal happiness, and the real world mission of the Belt and Road Initiative, as captured in a two-hour concert.

This Houston event was truly a contribution to a dialogue between cultures, sharing among the participants gifts of traditional and classical music from many parts of the world. Through these community concerts the Schiller Institute is unleashing an exchange of ideas, and giving voice to the shared principles of humanity, through expressions of profound beauty. We thereby illuminate the true purpose and reason to unify Mankind through the Belt and Road.

Schiller Institute/Dwight Jarrett
Sylvia Yan (left) and Amanda Cheung.

Ruling Party Foresees Attempt to Assassinate President Zuma

June 4—The ongoing, intense demonization of South African President Jacob Zuma is intended to create an environment in which his assassination would appear to be "the logical thing to do," said Deputy Finance Minister Sfiso Buthelezi on June 2, in delivering the keynote at a Cadres' Forum of the ruling African National Congress (ANC) in Pietermaritzburg, KwaZulu-Natal. He referred to Chris Hani having been demonized before his assassination in 1993. The killing of Hani, chief of staff of the ANC's armed wing, by the British Empire, would have led to a race war if Nelson Mandela had not made a strategic intervention, insisting that South Africans must remain calm.

Twitter/Presidency of South Africa

President Jacob Zuma presided at the launch of the first Trans-Africa locomotive on April 4, at state-owned enterprise Transnet, Pretoria. The Trans-Africa model is the first locomotive designed, engineered, and manufactured in Africa, but the event was scarcely mentioned in the British Empire-steered mass media in South Africa. Third and fourth from left are Minister of Public Enterprises Lynne Brown and President Zuma.

Buthelezi explained that Zuma had "touched the nerve of a powerful bloc" that was attempting to hold onto its economic power, although Buthelezi did not identify the British Empire in its current form as the beast to which he referred. The "powerful bloc," he said, is threatened by the Zuma government's plans for radical economic transformation, including the plan to spend $39 billion on infrastructure development.

Ongoing operations on behalf of the Empire by networks—including those of George Soros and Barack Obama—have assassination as an option.

This report updates the May 29 statement by R.P. Tsokolibane, leader of LaRouche South Africa, which follows.

The immediate background to Tsokolibane's statement is that President Zuma had come out on top on May 28, after the British faction in the ANC attempted, once again, to force his resignation. The confrontation took place at a three-day meeting of the party's ruling body, the 107-member National Executive Committee (NEC), in Pretoria. When some NEC members alleged that Zuma had been captured by private interests, Zuma told them that they were the ones who had been captured, clearly meaning that they were captives of a certain, unnamed "powerful bloc."

—David Cherry
dacherry3@yahoo.com

THE ENEMY IS THE BRITISH EMPIRE

Only the Smart Will Survive

May 28—I am pleased to see that President Zuma has prevailed against yet another attempt to oust him by the "regime changers" controlled by the British Empire and its assets in our country.

Let me state again clearly, for all sentient people to take notice: *the enemy of South Africa, its people, and the peoples of Africa, is the dying, but unfortunately not yet dead, British Empire*. That Empire—headed by the murderous and increasingly decrepit Royal Family and its bitch Queen—does not support any one leader here, or any particular group, but supports whatever it will take to deny South Africa its true destiny: to lead all of Africa out of the political and economic slavery of the City of London's global monetarist system, and into the bright future of peace and economic development.

That is the future that our great father, Nelson Mandela, envisioned, and as the great humanist and the world's leading physical economist, Lyndon LaRouche, has fought to bring into being for more than half a century. I am proud to fight shoulder to shoulder with Mr LaRouche and his wife Helga Zepp-LaRouche, the world famous "Silk Road Lady," for a new, just world economic order, in which humanity can finally rise to its greatest creative potential.

It is this new, emerging world order of peace, development, and justice for all peoples, that is the current, true enemy of the British Empire and its oligarchy. President Zuma, by throwing his support behind the initiatives of the BRICS nations—especially the China of President Xi and the Russia of President Putin—marks himself as an enemy combatant against the British Empire, whether he fully realizes it or not.

As my associates in the LaRouche movement have made clear in published reports, it is the British and their assets, such a former Nazi employee and speculator George Soros[1] and former American President Barack Obama, who unleashed and support the "regime changers" in our country, and elsewhere, in-cluding the attacks on the new American President, Donald Trump.

I warn President Zuma and all patriots who want to realize Mandela's vision for our country and for peace and prosperity for this continent: You cannot both support policies such as China's tremendous "One Belt, One Road" global infrastructure development plan, and at the same time compromise with the British Empire and its so-called "Commonwealth." The British oligarchs, however they may represent themselves, are like rabid dogs. They will infect and kill you, if you get close enough for them to bite.

Our nation is vital to the future of Africa in the emerging new paradigm coming from the East, which is embodied in the "One Belt, One Road" perspective. Despite our current economic problems, we are the only full-set economy on the continent, capable of producing the machines—and the machines to make those machines, called "machine tools"—that make development feasible. The successful implementation of the plans discussed at the recent, worldwide Belt and Road Forum—held in Beijing, May 14-15—will result in the British Empire and its global imperialist system collapsing into irrelevance, not only in the economic sense, but in the reality of the current and future.

For our nation to function, we must have a functioning and capable Presidency, which can carry out such initiatives as are needed to implement the economic program of the new paradigm. As I have stated before, the British policy is to make our nation ungovernable, to destroy not only our President, but the Presidency itself. We cannot let that happen!

A skirmish was won, once again, this weekend, but the battle rages on. It will not end until we and the world succeed in thrusting the British Empire into the dustbin of history where it belongs. I stand ready to assist in all ways possible in this great cause.

But we must be smart. Know your enemy and you can defeat him. Strike not at phantasms projected from behind a curtain of lies created by the Empire's media. Call our enemy by its right and proper name: The British Empire. Call its flunkies in our country the ass-lickers of the bitch Queen. Believe it or not, those simple acts will take us a long way forward on the road toward our ultimate victory.

—Ramasimong Phillip Tsokolibane
ramasimongt@hotmail.com

---

11. To understand the full depravity of George Soros, see this three-minute excerpt from a 1998 interview with him: https://www.youtube.com/watch?v=xPmKmfULrGI

III.

FEBRUARY 25, 1994

The Science of Physical Economy as The Platonic Epistemological Basis for All Branches of Human Knowledge

by Lyndon LaRouche

American statesman and physical economist Lyndon LaRouche wrote this document in 1994 after he was freed from prison on Jan. 26, 1994. He was a political prisoner for five years.

Beginning not long after 1989's economy-driven collapse of the Warsaw Pact system, gradually, those establishment thinkers who were no longer blinded by the hysterical mass-propaganda of the London- and Wall Street-centered monetarist financier factions have appeared to register publicly a fresh overview of what happened to the Soviet system at the close of the 1980s. Not only had the Warsaw Pact system disintegrated, but the collapse of the post-Yalta form of Anglo-Saxon financial and, probably, the political system, too, was not far behind. That succession of changes in economic policy introduced to the world's economy as a whole about 30 years ago, has set into motion a systemic disorder in the entire world's economy: a spiralling collapse of physical economy, a physical collapse caused by the insatiable appetites of an already vast, rapidly growing bubble of financial speculation, a systemic collapse-process comparable to a parasitical cancer feeding upon its dying victim.

Today, the only important economic policy-question confronting really intelligent thinkers in any other part of the world is: This financial system is doomed; can we put a new, healthy economic system into place in time to prevent the political disintegration of our nations which must tend to occur in the wake of the financial avalanche about to crush the world as a whole?

What confronts us thus is not one of your famous boom-bust, cyclical crises in financial markets; this is a systemic crisis, in which case, either the relevant economic policies are destroyed, or the economy is destroyed. Under these conditions, any attempt to divert the discussion of this matter by seeking to forecast the day, or even the month a final collapse might occur, would be a pathetic sort of diversionary exercise in irrelevance. As long as present, monetarist forms of "deregulation" and related "free trade" policies continue to be tolerated, it will be impossible to prevent a financial and economic collapse of entire nations. When? One should answer simply, that unless we eradicate the "free trade" and related policies which caused this crisis, a total collapse of the system will come all too soon. Under any continuation of the policies currently defended by Wall Street and the so-called neo-conservatives, these Anglo-Saxon monetarist policies of the recent 25 years, it is absolutely assured, that soon, the entire planet will be plunged into the worst financial and economic catastrophe which modern history could recall since analogous Venetian bankers' policies produced the mid-Fourteenth-century collapse of Europe.

In any case, even if last-minute policy-changes save the world from a breakdown of the physical economies, the existing world monetary and financial systems are doomed. Any economic recovery will depend upon the creation and unleashing of large-scale state-credit mechanisms which operate in freedom from an old system which will then exist only in the repose of bankruptcy reorganization.

Under such present conditions, it is more obviously urgent that we not measure the relative performance of economies by the monetary yardstick of currency prices, but by the reality of physical output and consumption of households, farms, and manufactures. If we examine the matter according to those physical standards of measurement, the world's economy, taken as a whole, has been, incontrovertibly, in a continuing, downward spiral of collapse since no later than 1971.

There is no natural cause for this economic decline of both the Anglo-American and former Soviet systems. In both cases, bad policy, not nature, is the culprit. The presently ongoing collapse of the post-Yalta economic order of the Anglo-Saxon alliance has been brought about through a quarter-century of wrong-headed choices of economic policy and science policy generally, wrong policies of virtually every government and other relevant institution of this planet. Bad policy, not nature is to blame for this. If one jumps from the roof of a two-story building and breaks one's leg, please have the decency not to file a tort claim against the law of gravity; it was the bad policies which have been defended, or tolerated up to this time by most among the putatively educated citizens of the United States and other nations, which are directly the cause for the holocaust of misery consuming this planet today.

EIRNS/Michael Micale

A scene in Houston, Texas. When a nation's physical economy does not provide families with the essential components of a household market-basket, what chance is there for children to become the scientists and explorers of the future?

1. Rudimentary Comparative Studies Of Physical-Economic Time-Series

First, let us highlight the proof of the argument, that a collapse has been in progress continuously over the past 40 years. After that interpolation, let us proceed, with helpful side-glances toward the recently published report on my 1948-52 discoveries in the science of physical economy, to show the kind of philosophical thinking which must be understood, practiced, and taught by the leading intelligentsia of nations, if the political institutions of those nations are not to be misled into disasters of the sort now pushing this entire planet into a prolonged New Dark Age.

Any person literate in either a branch of the physical sciences, or industrial cost accounting, could readily prove this post-1971 collapse to be an incontrovertible fact, using the relevant, available historical statistics. An opening summary of the thinking needed to construct a statistical demonstration of that fact will clear the way for presenting the central point of this report.

Since describing that computation is merely necessary background to the deeper issues of current policy-shaping, I shall outline the method of statistical construction as briefly and simply as the subject permits. To construct such measurements for the 1963-93 interval, we begin with a study of typical market-baskets of household consumption.

This includes the essentials of physical consumption, plus the two essential categories of services: health and education. The per-capita requirements for a household vary somewhat, of course. They vary according to the time in which the household is situated, and by the cultural level we are committed to achieving in practice through qualities of life-expectancy, health, rations of time allotted for education, and related development of both the household as a whole and the individual member, and so on.

What we require is a definition of a "standard household-consumption market-basket" based upon these elements. Let us ask ourselves, then: What is the kind of standard we require for comparing the case for different nations, or for the same or another nation in a different period of history? In practice, one should experiment with the changing statistics for any nation during a period of successful growth in both net domestic product and average standard of living: Examine the way in which actual household consumption varies according to both the economic-social characteristics of a household and its demographic composition. If one turns then to discussion of standard compositions of employment of a national labor-force in my textbook *So, You Wish to Learn All About Economics?* one should recognize the way in which one should proceed to construct a usable approximation of the standard required.

For example, prior to the eighteenth and nineteenth centuries' implementation of Leibniz's proposals for an industrial revolution based upon a system of heat-powered machinery whose technology was continually advancing, the existence of any society required that more than 90% of the labor force be employed in rural occupations. In contrast, if today's technology were generally used, with farm prices at the level we term "parity," less than 2% of a labor force is required in such modes of rural employment to satisfy abundantly the total population's needs for agricultural products. This improvement in productivity depends upon a prior and maintained supply of needed industrial goods to the farmer, and also a relevant development of elements of basic economic infrastructure which include rail transport, electrical power supplies, and generalized water man-

agement.

The solution to the problem of defining a refined standard of household market-basket first appears as we attempt to compare our approximations of market-basket standards for households with the market-basket requirements per capita of agricultural and industrial production of physical goods. One gains thus an insight into the fact of a correlation of such kind between per-capita productivity in production of goods, and per-capita consumption of the physical, health, and educational requirements of the households which, inclusively, provide production with its labor-force members.

Looking at the statistics from this standpoint, we conceptualize more easily the nature of the interdependence of productivity with the quality of per-capita and per-square-kilometer development of such forms of basic infrastructure as general transportation, water management, power supplies, sanitation, and basic urban infrastructure.

If we merely bear those kinds of analytical considerations in mind, the available U.N. and related statistics over the interval 1963-93 tell an incontrovertible story. In physical terms, over this period, the per-capita output of the total rural and urban labor force has been declining throughout the world as a whole; the fact that some regions of the world have been exceptional does not change the global picture (see **Figure 1**).

We can see, in this way, that the trend downward begins during the 1960s, with more and more suppression of the industrial development of nations in the southern hemisphere of this planet. The trend begins as an apparent slowing of the rate of economic growth, and then, during 1971-74, becomes an absolute decline in the so-called industrialized sector as a whole, in addition to the so-called developing sector. Even those national economies which do not go into absolute decline during the period 1971-81, are visibly affected by trends in the world around them. The overall condition of this planet during the 1980s is an uninterrupted, generally accelerating downward trend.

Let me speak of the relevant official and popular opinion in the United States. Similar observations are to be made on the subject of opinion in other countries. There are four principal reasons most people in the U.S.A. have been duped into accepting false 1980s or more recent reports of "economic recovery," or even "prosperity."

First, there is the credulity of the majority of the

FIGURE 1
World Output 1961-91

Tons per worker

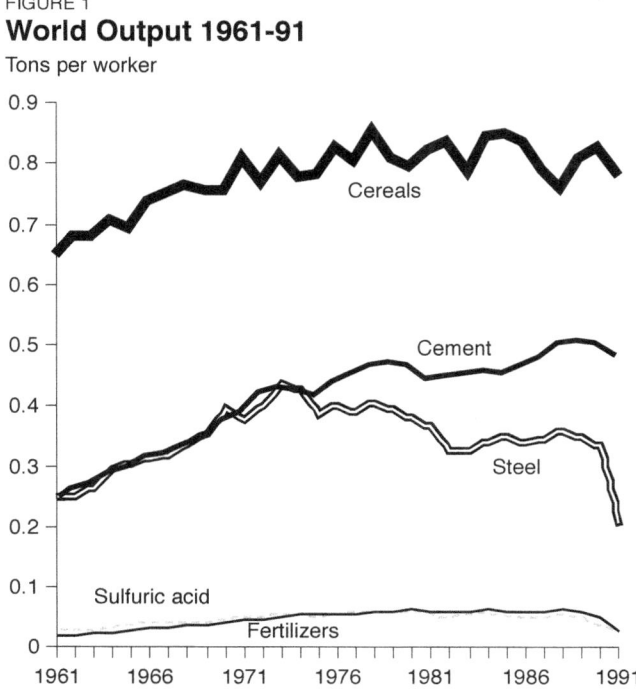

Source: FAO Rome, UNICPS

U.S. population today.

The influential Fabian Walter Lippmann proposed a Goebbels-like mass-media brainwashing of Americans in his famous book on public opinion; to similar effect and purpose, David Riesman made infamous the pathetic type of Twentieth-century North American which he named an "other-directed" personality. Hannah Arendt, the one-time lover of the Nazi regime's chief Nietzschean philosopher Martin Heidegger, proposed that anyone who did not fit the model of this brainwashed, "politically correct," other-directed type should be ostracized as what she termed an "authoritarian personality." The average American, including the shallow-minded, highly suggestible "populist type," has come to accept whatever themes are currently implicit in addictive forms of mass-spectator sports, Hollywood entertainment, popular quasi-music, and the mass news media, as axiomatically the basis for constructing one's own "socially acceptable" forms of participation in "politically correct" forms of mass opinion.

Repeat often enough, Goebbels-style, that the basis of economy is "free competition in the market-place," that economy is ruled by a mythical "law of supply and demand," or the popularized lie that the U.S. Constitution was based upon John Locke, or the lie that the young U.S. federal economy was founded upon the ideas of Adam Smith, and the "other-directed" type of American will regurgitate that nonsense ritually as if he believed that were the holiest of eternal verities.

An included factor, the collapse of the quality of U.S. education, especially under the influence of Fabians and kindred types, such as John Dewey and his followers, had already damaged seriously the cognitive development of nearly all Americans even before the application of such New Age concoctions as the radical positivist "New Math" and other destructive innovations of the recent three decades.

The development of the cognitive capabilities of the young to the degree needed for a pro-scientific, rigorous quality of independent judgment, usually appears only through the form of education rooted in the Greek and later Classics, and emphasizing for instruction in mathematics, biology, and physics the student's re-experiencing the original act of each important axiomatic-revolutionary discovery of his or her forebears. The misguided substitution of the textbook, and of generally accepted algebraic formalisms as a replacement for wrestling with Classical and other original sources has produced predominantly a type of graduate, even among those burdened with terminal scientific degrees, which Friedrich Schiller named contemptuously *Brotgelehrten* (bread scholars).

The result of substituting behaviorist modes of "learning" for development of independent cognitive powers of rigorous original discovery, has produced, among typical academic and other strata, a virtually total lack of capacity for independent thinking, especially respecting axiomatic qualities of assumption. This moral defect of judgment is often seen in its most extreme form in precisely those moments that an American asserts most loudly his "independent judgment" on a matter. Thus, do such foolish conceits of disordered public opinion render the politically correct true believer the better suited to be a victim of the silly opinions he or she is induced thus to adopt.

Second, current statistical practice of national-income accounting by governmental agencies, and by other widely influential reporting agencies, disallows any efforts at a rational distinction between a physically useless expansion of nominal income and useful production and consumption. For example, if prostitution and drug-trafficking were legalized, over $500 billion would be added to officially reported Gross National

FIGURE 2
U.S. Gross Domestic Product, and Services Portion of GDP

(in billion of dollars)

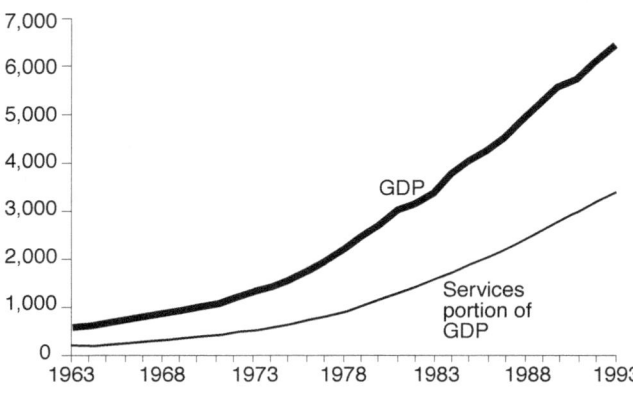

Source: U.S. Department of Commerce

Gross Dosmestic Product ia a fake concept. Between 1963 and 1993, fed by speculation, United States GDP rose from $603.1 billion, to a level of $6,374.0. During this period, Services as a component of GDP rose from, 39% to 54%, but even 'non-services' growth represented a huge element of fraud. During this period, when GDP allegedly rose 10-fold, sectors of the real physical economy were actually contracting between 30 and 50% or more, on a per-household and per-capita basis

TABLE 1
Declining Installation of Turbine Generator Capacity by U.S. Electric Utiities

Year	Installed capacity (megawatts)	Per capita (watts)	Per household (watts)	Per km² (watts)
1969	22,291	109.9	358.2	2378.3
1970	27,741	135.2	437.5	2959.7
1971	26,087	125.6	405.2	2783.3
1972	31,924	152.0	478.7	3406.0
1973	35,392	167.0	518.5	3776.1
1974	36,397	170.1	521.0	3883.3
1975	34,440	159.4	484.2	3674.5
1976	20,421	93.6	280.2	2178.7
1977	27,525	124.9	371.0	2936.7
1978	22,729	102.1	298.9	2425.0
1979	17,195	76.4	222.3	1834.6
1980	22,406	98.3	277.3	2390.5
1981	15,177	65.9	184.2	1619.2
1982	13,236	56.9	158.4	1412.2
1983	10,032	42.7	119.5	1070.3
1984	19,730	83.3	231.0	2105.0
1985	17,108	71.6	197.1	1825.3
1986	16,065	66.7	181.6	1714.0
1987	11,443	47.0	127.8	1220.8
1988	8,068	32.8	88.5	860.8
1989	7,312	29.5	78.7	780.1
1990	4,504	18.0	47.6	480.5

Source: Edison Electric Institute.

Product (GNP), without any actual increase in anything but the credulity of the suggestible cohorts within the population (see **Figure 2**). Thus, a vast, parasitical burgeoning of notional values of financial gains in various purely speculative forms is counted as national income on the same basis as production of food, clothing, education, medical care, bridges, tunnels, railways, and industrial workplaces. As long as the nominal income from parasitical sources such as financial speculation is nominally greater in price than the margin of collapse of infrastructure, producers and households' goods, the official idiot-savants of the statistical and mass media communities will continue to insist, with a fanatic's menacing gleam in their eyes, that our national economy is either at the brink of recovery, or even being "overheated by an excessive rate of growth"!

Third, over all of the past quarter-century, but especially the recent decade, the official statisticians have lied more and more shamelessly, on almost every subject, most of the time. In addition, they have refused to deduct from gross national incomes the cost represented by the failure to repair and maintain essential elements of basic economic infrastructure, such as rail-way systems, highways, bridges, water management systems, power stations and grids, and so on (see **Table 1**). In the United States, many trillions of dollars of never-existing "value added" have been added routinely, cumulatively, to construct false, greatly inflated reports of annual U.S. GNP.

Fourth, since the Ford Foundation's fraudulent, but influential *Triple Revolution* report of 1964, that doctrine of "post-industrial" utopianism has produced a malignant growth in the percentile of the total U.S. labor force which is either unemployed, about 17% or more today, or is employed in forms of "services" which add virtually nothing, or even less than nothing to either the net physical product-output or productivity of the U.S. economy (see **Figure 3**). Although most of the non-productive service occupations, as in the "fast food" distributorships, are paid wages way below the level required to support a household decently, the aggregate inflationary cost of these "services" is monstrous. The worst, the most savagely parasitical, are legalized gambling, recreational (illegal) drug-trafficking, and financial services.

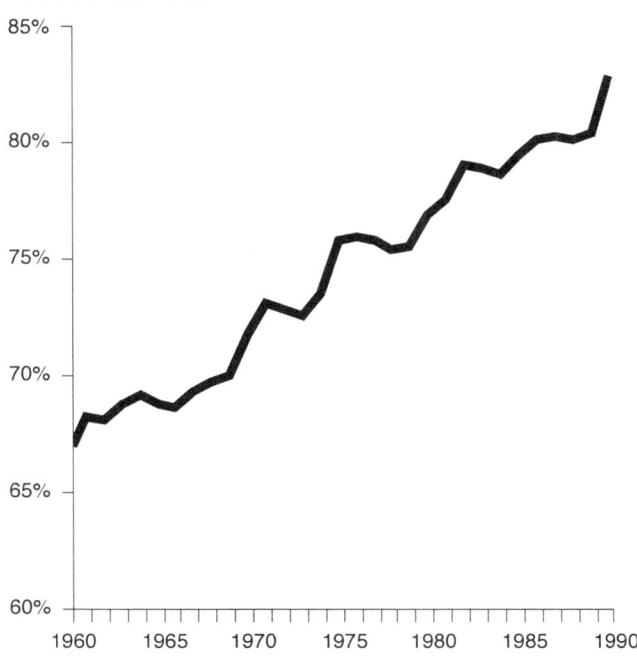

FIGURE 3
U.S. Overhead Employment 1960-90
Percent of labor force

It ought to be plain enough, as a matter of relatively simple calculations, that such a replacement of productive employment by services is intrinsically a form of inflationary rot which must destroy the nation in the end, if the policy is not reversed. Yet, babbling so-called "experts," whether as "talking heads" on the television screen, or elsewhere, have induced a majority of Americans to "repeat after me: The modern form of economy is a post-industrial, services economy." The Wall Street emperor has no clothes!—but, the credulous crowd of onlookers to that paraded nakedness shouts its admiration of the marvelous fabrics and tailoring.

Credulous popular opinion aside, the scientific importance of stressing the pathological side of expanded rations of services employment is illustrated conveniently in the following way.

Up to modern times—in other words, up to about 550 years ago, even as recently as 300 years ago—over 90% of the population must labor in the rural life, simply to keep the whole society from collapse into mortal want. The margin of decrease of the required rural percentile of the labor force, which technological progress has made possible, was absorbed chiefly by a smaller but, initially, nearly proportionate increase in two categories of physical-productive employment: the

building and maintaining of basic economic infrastructure and the direct production of useful physical necessities for consumption by individual households or industries. President George Washington's treasury secretary, Alexander Hamilton, accurately forecast this coordinate growth of urban industry and rural productivity in his famous official 1791 report to Congress, his outline of the anti-Adam Smith "American System of Political Economy" upon which our constitutional federal republic was founded, his *On the Subject of Manufactures.*

Also, in addition to the growth of the percentile of the labor force employed in urban production of physical goods, modern history's successive transformations in the "structure" of employment have been accompanied by an, aggregately, relatively smaller margin of employment distributed among four categorical "overhead" elements of social cost which are not explicitly, directly productive of physical output or goods or infrastructure: education, health care, science and technology per se, and administration.

In general, the change into these directions, from the old, pre-industrial, bucolic base, is associated with three correlated developments: increase in per-capita physical productivity of operatives, increasing complexity of the social division of labor, and increase of power-flux-density. Among the principal other features of these directions in structural change of labor-force composition, we have the following. The absolute increase in level of technology, combined with the rate of that increase requires an increase of the segment of employment assigned to science and technology as such. The educational requirement is increased similarly, both cumulatively and with respect to the rate of technological progress. The educational and related culture requirements of the household members place a premium upon prolonging healthy longevity of the population, and what that implies otherwise. Justifiable increase in administrative burdens is chiefly a reflection of the growth of industry, education, scientific progress, and health requirements. Also, a continual increase in physical productivity, per capita and per square kilometer, correlates with an increase of the ratio of employment in producers' goods production to employment in households' goods production.

One point to be singled out here, is the danger of exceeding justified levels of administrative employment. The combination of unjustified burgeoning of sales and administration expenses, plus growth of re-

TABLE 2
Production Levels for Goods in Producers' and Consumers' Market-baskets on a Per-household basis (1967=1.000)

	1967	1973	1979	1982	1990
Consumers' market-basket					
Men's trousers	1.000	0.965	0.594	0.504	0.335
Men's shirts	1.000	0.644	0.486	0.343	0.165
Women's blouses	1.000	1.023	1.511	1.405	0.684
Women's dresses	1.000	0.597	0.503	0.339	0.279
Woven woollens	1.000	0.264	0.254	0.139	0.166
Refrigerators	1.000	1.247	0.935	0.703	0.932
Passenger cars	1.000	1.150	0.869	0.484	0.512
Tires	1.000	1.020	0.833	0.666	0.877
Radios	1.000	0.706	0.467	0.316	0.098
Producers' market-basket					
Metal-cutting machine tools	1.000	0.643	0.530	0.289	0.212
Metal-forming machine tools	1.000	0.854	0.730	0.404	0.406
Bulldozers	1.000	1.200	0.713	0.334	0.306
Graders and levellers	1.000	0.786	0.748	0.383	0.349
Pumps	1.000	1.140	0.541	0.424	0.506
Steel	1.000	1.029	0.821	0.416	0.487
Intermediate goods for either market-basket					
Gravel and crushed stone	1.000	1.023	0.914	0.624	0.575
Clay	1.000	1.022	0.759	0.459	0.544
Bricks	1.000	0.999	0.850	0.451	0.598
Cement	1.000	1.045	0.911	0.632	0.689

A production level for each item for 1967 was determined, and then divided by the number of households in 1967. This yielded a production level on a per household basis. For example, in 1967, the United States had 59,236,000 households and produced 86,014 metal-cutting machine tools. Thus, there were 0.001452 metal-cutting machine tools produced per household. The 1967 level was set equal to 1, and all subsequent years' production levels were compared to it. By 1990, the United States produced but 0.000308 metal-cutting machine tools per household, a level that was only 21.2% of what it was in 1967.

During 1967-90, production levels, on a per household basis for major goods contained in both the producers and consumers' market baskets fell between 7 and 90%, with most goods registering a collapse of 40% or more. This represents a fall in both the producers and consumers' market baskets as a whole, and shows the inability of the United States to reproduce itself.

dundant employment in questionable expansion of so-called "services," is an inflationary economic disorder akin to cancer in living processes, a sickness which could ultimately bring about the death of economies—as it has been slowly, but visibly killing the U.S. economy during the past 40 irrational years of continued drift into post-industrial utopianism.

Once the implications of these observations are grasped, the usefulness of the following, somewhat simplified approach to comparative statistical analysis should be intelligible.

For estimating the relative growth or collapse of a national economy, or world economy over successive years, or decades, a good rough estimate can be made in the following way.

Make all measurements in terms of per-capita, per-household, and per-square-kilometer values. Measure basic economic infrastructure, agriculture, mining, industry (manufacturing, construction other than infrastructure), and employment in education, science and technology as such, and health-care. Measure consumption and production, coherently, as follows: market-baskets of household consumption (physical plus health, education), per household, per square kilometer and per capita; market-baskets of producers' goods, consumed and produced, per capita, per square kilometer and per household; ratios of producers' goods to household goods turnover, per capita, per square kilometer, and per household (see **Table 2**).

In examining these statistics, take special note of the following consideration. Distinguish between the productivity of labor as measured, on the one side, with respect to monetary price of direct labor employed, and, on the other side, productivity as physical economy measures it, the latter in terms of comparable physical ("market-basket") units of output. For example, in physical economy, measure the percentile of the total labor force of a nation required to sustain the essential contents of a household market-basket for all members of that labor force.

In the first, monetary case, a rough, first-approximation measurement is as follows. One subtracts from the wholesale manufacturer's price of produced goods sold, the price-cost of materials consumed by that production; this yields a difference, a gross margin, corresponding roughly to nominal (monetary) "value added by production." In the second case, we make a formally analogous rough measurement, substituting physical market-baskets of inputs and outputs of production; this defines a physical margin of "value added" per capita, per household, and per square kilometer. Let us concentrate now solely upon the physical measurement, in opposition to the monetary one.

First, refine the rough physical measurement. Let us make that physical margin of "value added" the numer-

Migrant laborers pick beans in New York. The "downsizing" of the productive sector, as corporations search for "cheap labor" at home and abroad, is a disastrous strategy for the U.S. economy.

USDA-C&MS Photo

ator of a fraction; make the denominator the total physical investment, per capita of labor force, in household and related consumption by productive labor, and of materials and physical capital of production. This calculation yields a useful estimation of productive "return on investment," in physical, non-monetary terms. One obvious advantage of this enhanced estimation is, that it reflects more accurately the relationship between productivity at a local point of production and the productivity of the national economy's productive sector as a whole.

To render such physical output comparable with physical input, we reduce each to its labor-content. This content is reflected, in first approximation, by hours of direct productive labor consumed in production. These raw hours, for each case of an item in the market-basket list, are corrected by an adjustment-factor. This compares the households' market-basket of consumption of the actual direct labor employment in production of an item, with a standard consumption. That standard consumption is obtained by averaging total national consumption of direct labor's households with the total number of direct labor employed in the nation. This provides a mean value of consumption per capita of direct labor for the average household of direct labor. That tactic provides the indexing of the actual case required. The mean-hour of industrial-engineering type of cost-accounting is indexed for each type of production in this way.

Thus, it might appear to some Cambridge systems analyst who is thinking carelessly, or to a like-minded student of the input-output schemes of Wassily Leontief, that we are treating this as a case of apparent production of commodities by commodities consumed. In fact, we are employing such an assumption merely to refute it: The fact that when commodities are consumed by direct productive labor, apparently the commodities are modally reproducing themselves negentropically, reflects the function of labor, as distinguished from any other form of consumption of produced items. Implicitly, we are refuting directly the famous axiomatic assumption of the Eighteenth-century French and Swiss Physiocrats. It is only the labor process which can impose willfully such forms of negentropic, or should we better say "evolutionary-type" transformations of functional processes to a higher state. This is adumbration of Genesis 1:26-28 as shown by the modal form of a durably successive form of society.

By taking the ratio of the activity of the productive sector's labor-force households to the physical costs and income, per household, of the nation as a whole, a useful estimate of relative national productivity is obtained.

We may thus compare different nations, and the same nations during different periods: both in terms of their respective productive sectors, and the results of relating each productive sector to the nation as a whole in this way.

1.1 The Myth of 'Cheap Labor'

This approach to estimating relative productivity of nations provides a simple, implicitly conclusive exposure of the fraud in British economist David Ricardo's celebrated myth of a "comparative advantage" allegedly inhering in "cheap labor." Our view of today's widespread "free trade" delusion affords us a better approximation of the actual process of this past 20-odd

FIGURE 4

Productive Labor, People and Workers

United States 1960-90

years of the worldwide economic-collapse spiral.

On behalf of the proposition that a U.S. corporation, for example, should situate a new manufacturing plant in some underdeveloped nation noted for its favorable tax climate and supply of cheap labor, today's Wall Street financial houses console the North Americans who will lose their employment in this way: "If you wish to stop your jobs from flying away to cheap-labor markets, you have only to lower your wage-expectations to levels which are competitive with foreign competition." Similarly, in the university economics departments, the spin-doctors will assure all foolish enough to believe them, that cheaper imports from foreign sources are a boon to the U.S. consumer, and therefore a boon to the U.S. economy as a whole.

Imports are an actual boon to the U.S. economy, for example, under different circumstances than those referenced by such academic spin-doctors. If a technologically developed economy can move its culturally developed labor out of low-skilled employment into more highly productive, more technologically advanced modes of production, the total and per-capita productivity of the whole U.S. economy is increased to everyone's advantage. Thus, if we assign the less-skilled forms of market-basket item to a nation whose labor

force has yet to reach generally the level of the U.S. labor force, we are benefitting both nations by optimizing the utilization of the labor force of the less-developed nation, and maximizing the productivity of the relatively more developed one.

The directly opposite result would be the case if we moved chunks of the employed U.S. labor force either into unemployment status, or into less-skilled, lower-paid employment, or out of production of physical goods into services employment. In the former case, the U.S. economy would have the added production and income to be a market for the product of the developing nation; in the latter case, the purchasing power of U.S. households would be reduced, and, therefore, also the U.S. market as a whole.

In that reality which appears to exist only outside the mouths of free-trade ideologues, the effect of the "runaway shop," under today's post-industrial policies, is to shrink the percentile of the total U.S. labor force employed in producing useful physical goods. The displaced labor from these runaway industrial enterprises becomes either unemployed or employed in relatively marginal, even essentially almost useless occupations. The industrial purchases from U.S. suppliers, especially medium and smaller producers and maintenance services, collapse. The tax revenue base of the affected community is collapsed more or less severely. The "downsizing" of the per-capita scale of the U.S. agro-industrial producers' base, and the "downsizing" of the percentile of the total U.S. labor force employed in production of physical goods, signifies a collapsing of the U.S. economy's earned real purchasing power, and a collapsing of the U.S. economy below a physical break-even point (see **Figure 4**).

In consequence of this and other policies born of the same deranged, if media-popularized mind-set, we have the following picture of the U.S. economy itself.

Over the interval 1965-70, the rate of growth of the U.S. physical economy slowed toward a net zero growth for the economy as a whole (in terms of rate of increase of physical output per capita, per household, per square kilometer). The slowdown was triggered by the "downsizing" of the highly stimulative, "post-Sputnik" aerospace "crash program" and investment tax-credit programs upon which the post-1960 economic recovery from the 1957-60 recession had depended almost entirely. This "downsizing" was worsened by the combined influence of such "post-modernist" lunacies as Robert Theobald's *Triple Revolution,* Robert S. McNamara's lunatic "systems analysis," Herbert Marcuse's ultra-leftism, and sundry "post-industrial" utopianisms. The international effects of these and similar "New Age" policies led to Prime Minister Harold Wilson's November 1967 collapse of British sterling, and the ensuing first round of successive collapses of the U.S. dollar erupting visibly during February and early March 1968.

During 1970-71, the U.S. net expenditure on basic economic infrastructure (additions and replacements versus wear, tear, and obsolescence) entered a phase of negative growth which has not only continued, but accelerated downward to the present time. The resulting repair bill for water-management systems, transportation systems, power systems, general sanitation, and urban infrastructure generally now totals many trillions of dollars at constant-dollar prices. The combined Chrysler and Penn Central crises of spring 1970 signalled the next round of collapse of the U.S. dollar, leading to the collapse of the Bretton Woods gold reserve system during March through Aug. 15, 1971.

The further downsizing of the U.S. productive sector by the Nixon administration's successive, so-called "Phase I" and "Phase II," was followed, during 1973 and 1974, by the shockingly depressive effects of Secretary of State Henry A. Kissinger's arranging the OPEC oil-price hoax on behalf of the London-based oil multis, then known popularly as the "Seven Sisters." This disastrous direction in U.S. domestic and foreign economic and related policy and trends was accelerated by adoption of those sets of policies sponsored by David Rockefeller's Trilateral Commission and the New York Council on Foreign Relations' "Project 1980s." These included the "shock therapy" measures introduced by President Carter's newly appointed Federal Reserve chairman, Paul A. Volcker, in October 1979. Volcker's high-interest rate hoax, which had been put forward first in the CFR "Project 1980s," and backed by the Trilateral lobbyists, had an immediately catastrophic effect upon the U.S. economy. Thus, over the course of the 1970s as a whole, the U.S. economy collapsed in all productive sectors excepting a few electronic and related spin-offs of the Kennedy aerospace program; the rate of contraction of the U.S. and world economy, over the course of the 1980s was transformed into a virtually terminal collapse-process by the Anglo-American policies of 1985-92, especially those introduced by Margaret Thatcher and George Bush.

TABLE 3

Water use for industrial purposes, 1970 (millions of cubic meters per year)

	per household	per capita
United States	950	294
Germany	470	170
Japan	500	128
India	30	6
China	50	11

A critical feature of an economy's real economic development is its ability to supply itself with water. In 1970, the difference between three industrial nations (the United States, Germany, and Japan) and two developing sector nations (India and China) was significant. On a per household basis, the industrial nations deployed between 10 and 20 times the water to industry as the developing sector nations .. on a per capita basis, the disparity was even greater. Lawfully, this resulted, in part, in much higher industrial output in the industrial nations.

"Downsizing" has become an irrationalist, fanatical cult. This popular myth currently includes the delusion, that one could collapse 85% of this planet into plague-ridden barbarism, during a time as long as a century, and yet keep a residual 15% of this planet relatively secure and stable. This delusion is closely related to the false axiomatic assumptions underlying the popularized fallacy known as "comparative advantage" of "low taxes and cheap labor."

The ability to continue to produce physical goods of ever-better quality ever-more cheaply is an excellent, indispensable policy. This realization of this praiseworthy goal demands a constant emphasis upon investment in improved technologies generated by vigorous scientific progress in such directions as beyond the outer limits of present-day astrophysics and microphysics. This improvement in conditions of life also depends upon essential considerations of basic economic infrastructure; this requirement cannot be compromised without disastrous effects upon the economy.

In transport, for example: the promptness and cheapness of inbound and outbound passengers and freight. Availability of reliable water supplies (see **Table 3**). Availability of adequate power supplies of the required quality. Local communications. Sanitation. Education and health-care systems. Apart from that class of correlatives, a potential level of per-capita physical productivity is principally a function of health and cultural development of the labor force.

In all cases, these qualities of the local situation for

investment in production must be produced chiefly by, and at the cost of the society in which the investment is made. Either that society is able (and willing) to reproduce these required "environmental" preconditions, or it is politically unwilling to do so. If it is willing to do so, then that society as a whole must be repaid amounts sufficient to regenerate those improvements. Even were it willing, it might be incapable of doing so. If a large number of investors in a country pay so cheaply for their employed labor, and so forth, that the country is strained beyond the limit of its means to continue to reproduce these required "environmental" conditions, then a spiral of collapse is introduced by cheap-labor, low-tax fostering of such investments.

Otherwise, if the so-called "cheap labor region" in which the investment is made is paid generally sufficient tax revenues and wage-levels to enable it those necessary preconditions, then the labor in that nation will no longer be truly "cheap." As the legacy of Eighteenth-century Dutch and British colonialism, and Nineteenth-century British imperialism show throughout the relevant southerly regions of this planet, the "comparative advantage" of cheap slave or paid colonial labor lies entirely in the power of the colonialist to conduct a mass-murderous, Nazi occupation-like type of asset-stripping of the population and natural resources of the subjugated region.

Thus, it is a matter of economic principle, that the true cost of producing anything, including the public sector's contributions of general, national infrastructure, must be seen as the physical cost of reproducing and improving all of those natural and developed resources upon which the continued local production, even by a localized investment, of an equal or greater quantity and quality depends. Among the included actually incurred costs of an investment: each local investment in production must contribute its share to meeting the reproduction costs of the total population from whose households the labor employed is drawn.

EIRNS/Stuart Lewis

British-style free trade in action: the "street economy" in New York City. The unscientific axiomatic assumptions of the British East India Company's Haileybury school are now generally accepted in ruling academic institutions around the world.

'Asset-Stripping'

Since the mid-1960s turn, the U.S. financier interest has adapted to that induced physical collapse of the U.S. economy which its post-industrial policy has induced, responding to this collapse with an increasing emphasis upon sundry forms of asset-stripping. We should understand "asset-stripping" as various ways in which to make a financial profit by acquiring physical or monetary assets for resale by purchasing them at a price way below the replacement price for the physical assets underlying the notional financial values assigned to them. "Junk bond" dealings are one example of such looting. It will probably be helpful to many readers to present the following, additional example of commonplace "asset-stripping" practices.

In a typical case, a banker linked to the organized crime circles formerly run top-down by Meyer Lansky assists a credulous client's investment today, but with the intent to loot him at some point down the line—make the calf happy with today's fattening, that he might become a richer feast the day he is driven into the asset-stripping slaughterhouse. One day, often years later, after the investment has been "fattened up" by aid of what seemed to have been generously supplied masses of credit, one of the creditors, not the original banker, mysteriously calls in a loan. Other things happen. The client is thrown into bankruptcy. His former patron, the banker, with an interest in the enterprise all along, buys out the other creditors by taking the assets at one or two dimes' worth for each dollar of replacement cost of those assets, and readily disposes of the assets so acquired for three or more dimes, at a 50% or greater profit in the relatively short term. In typical real instances of such widespread practices, this buyout of the bankrupted assets occurs by looting the original investor, the bank depositors of relevant banks, and sundry other creditors.

That and analogous forms of monetarist "downsizing" within an existing local, national, or world economy, generates a relatively substantial, if local rate of return, substantial relative to the notional value of base being shrunken physically by these means. One way of accomplishing this result, is to send a "runaway shop" into a cheap-labor market, to loot both the market and the basis of that national economy out of which the "runaway shop" has been wrenched. The already-referenced "junk bonds" are the same species of asset-stripping rip-off; so are "derivatives." The London and Wall Street private bankers do not invest in cheap labor for the purpose of obtaining wealth from production; the only significant source of wealth from such operations is the wealth taken from a domain outside the production process itself, the looting of the host economy by the levers of exchange manipulations and of tax- and price-concessions. In short, this is accomplished through an asset-stripping operation, in which the production side serves only as a lever.

Another form of asset-stripping, is arbitrarily lowering the birth rate. The ability to maintain the whole economy on the same scale requires a reproduction of the labor force in that or an increased number of surviving post-adolescents of a suitable quality of cognitive development and health. For example, by eliminating new births altogether, or virtually so, one could lower the level of income required, per capita, to reduce the number of mouths to be fed sufficiently to reach temporarily an otherwise impossible level of market basket enjoyed by the survivors of this population-collapse spiral: Labor-force members from households without dependent children are much cheaper to employ, since they have fewer mouths to feed per member of the labor force (see **Figure 5**).

Similarly, by putting health-caps upon care for per-

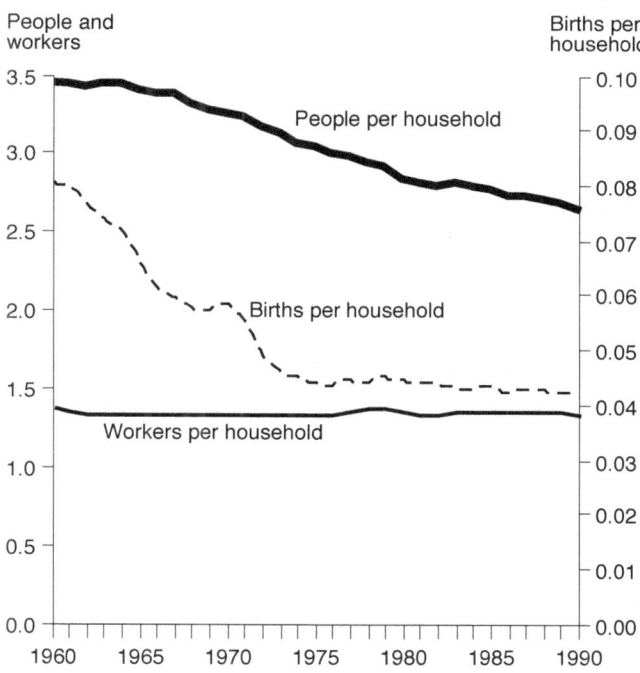

FIGURE 5
Household Composition 1960-90

sons whose age is above 55 years, one could eliminate, Hitler-style, most of the older strata of the total population; this would lower the income required by the survivors, per capita, to maintain the current standard of living for the survivors. The significance is, that to have a population which could afford to provide the existing middle-range U.S. standard of income per capita, a population which describes an infant-based demographic pyramid with a modal life expectancy of up to 85 or more years, is required.

It was inevitable, that once the neo-malthusian fanatics had succeeded in their goals of dropping the birth-rate and introducing a "post-industrial" utopia, the Orwellian goal of killing off large fractions of persons who reach the age of retirement must be seen by the malthusians as the economically required next step. Reducing the birth-rate means reducing the economic basis for sustaining persons in retirement age-ranges. All "life-boat economics" of this sort, fairly called "Hitler-style economic policies," have an analogous effect.

The use of asset-stripping forms of "privatization" of public education, combined with outcome-based education's (OBE) emphasis on eliminating compulsory public education of cognitive potentials, is also an "asset-stripping" form of forerunner for Hitler-like healthcare and other population-control measures tomorrow. Without a form of obligatory public education which emphasizes European civilization's classics and a geometrical approach to development of the cognitive potentials, the result converges upon a deranged population reminiscent of Fourteenth-century European flagellant mobs, a population incapable of mastering the standards of technological proficiency required by modern agriculture and industry.

None of these "lower taxes," "cheaper labor" forms of asset-stripping are truly sustainable forms of cost-control measures. They are, each and all, essentially one-time modes of deriving income from mass-murderous forms of asset-stripping of the accumulated physical and cultural wealth of our collapsing society.

Thus, in order to discover the approximate degree of post-1963 declines, during, respectively, the 1960s, the 1970s, the 1980s, and the early 1990s, one must consider first the apparent levels of output per capita, per household, and per square kilometer. One must deduct from this apparent output the amount of current physical wealth attributable to the various guises of asset-stripping.

The additional considerations to be applied to the statistics are presented in my referenced 1984 textbook. That taken into account, you have before you the outlines of construction for an incontrovertible statistical proof: Since 1963, the world economy has been declining in net production of wealth per capita, per household, and per square kilometer. This rate of decline has itself been increasing over that period, most emphatically the past ten years.

2.0 Smith, Ricardo, and Marx: British Imperialism's Zero-growth Economists

During 1983-85, I forecast repeatedly, both in private and widely distributed published statements, an approximately 1988 collapse of the Warsaw Pact economic system, should Moscow refuse to reject the form of cooperation which President Reagan had proposed in his initial presentations of a Strategic Defense Initiative (SDI) offer delivered publicly on March 23, 1983. I also warned, similarly, from 1983 onwards, that under Anglo-American policies in force then and now, that the western economic system was also headed toward a

systemic form of collapse far worse than any mere cyclical depression. During the October 1988 U.S. presidential campaign, I warned a nationwide U.S. television audience of such things as the impending threat of a generalized Balkan war launched by certain Serbia factions, and also forecast an impending, early reunification of Germany under conditions of an imminent "East bloc" chain-reaction collapse. The collapse of the former Soviet system erupted in 1989; the intrinsically bankrupt Anglo-American financial system is now wobbling at the edge of a precipice.

The collapse of both systems was set into motion by policies introduced globally chiefly since the November 1963 assassination of President John F. Kennedy. The common feature of this past 20-odd years collapse of both of the planet's dominant economic systems, the Anglo-American and the Soviet, is that, in both cases, the collapse was shaped chiefly by common defects of policy-shaping thinking. These defects are rooted axiomatically in the British East India Company's Haileybury school of Adam Smith, Jeremy Bentham, David Ricardo, et al.

To understand why and how the world's economy entered the past 30 years collapse-spiral, one must recognize that this collapse has been caused solely by the influence of those ideas of zero-growth economy which were embedded axiomatically in the thinking of Adam Smith and Karl Marx, and, more recently, in the "systems analysis" introduced to post-1938 economics by radical positivist John Von Neumann. One also must recognize that, contrary to popular opinion, economist Karl Marx was a follower of this British school in every relevant sense, not merely an admirer of what he so often alleged to be the unchallenged scientific superiority of that Smith-Ricardo school. It is also a relevant fact that, virtually all of his adult life, through 1871, Marx was a controlled asset of two of the principal control agents of Lord Palmerston's foreign-intelligence service: London resident Giuseppe Mazzini and the British "Museum's" chief controller of Marx's education in economics, David Urquhart.

For the purposes of this report, we are interested only in a narrower aspect of Palmerston's control over Marx. Although his work on economics is usually associated with the notion of "surplus value," in every feature of the formal argument throughout the three volumes of his *Capital,* he is, mathematically, a zero-growth economist. On this point, there is no axiomatic difference between Marx and those whom he repeatedly acknowledged as his teachers, notably Smith and Ricardo. We stress that, as some postwar Cambridge University economists around Joan Robinson and Nicholas Kaldor have indicated, the formal side of Marx's *Capital* is readily restated as a relatively more sophisticated version of Von Neumann's zero-growth "systems analysis," that is, as a system of linear inequalities.

Kaldor's Cambridge Systems Analysis group, working closely with the malthusian Zuckerman-Alexander King Club of Rome, plainly influenced the direction of Soviet economic policy-thinking during the 1970s and early 1980s. That influence, exerted through such channels as Lord Solly Zuckerman and Dzherman Gvishiani's International Institute for Applied Systems Analysis in Laxenburg, Austria, did not cause the Soviet economic collapse; nonetheless, to those who observed this influence during that time, IIASA's conduiting of British systems-analysis influences into Moscow through that and other channels certainly blinded many relevant Soviet figures to the true causes of the catastrophe then in the making.

On the Anglo-American side of the collapse, the connection to Adam Smith is simple and direct. Radical versions of Smith's dogma are embodied axiomatically in the policy-thinking which is bringing the Anglo-American financial system to an early systemic collapse.

To understand such specific connection of bad economic theory to systemic collapse, we now treat in succession two successive, interrelated points. The first of these is the way in which the underlying assumptions of British economics dogma, since the eighteenth century, became rooted in today's policies of most governments and universities throughout the world. Secondly, we must examine rigorously the axiomatic connection between certain classes of ideas and material effects of those ideas in economic practice. The crucial economic implications of modern systems analysis, including the manner in which this radical version of Smith, Ricardo, Marx et al. has shaped the presently ongoing global economic collapse, can be understood only from that twofold standpoint.

In both of those facets of this subject-matter, the most crucial feature of this is the fact that the formal side of the economics teachings influencing both western and Soviet policy-shaping was derived from a doctrine whose formalities tolerate no economic policies which are not consistent with a zero-growth result.

Review briefly the definition of axiomatics. Later, we shall identify how the unscientific axiomatic assumptions of the British East India Company's Haileybury school became generally accepted in ruling Twentieth-century academic institutions around the world.

2.1 Axiomatics, Briefly

Let us be certain that we understand one another when we use the term "axiomatics." Stated most simply, we mean what the classic text in Euclidean geometry defines "axiom" to signify in practice. Unfortunately, there are many university science graduates today who, as victims of the so-called "New Math" curriculum introduced 30 years ago, were denied a competent grounding in geometry. Those who did receive such a grounding will please kindly bear with us as the meaning of the term is explained to those who did not.

Fairly said: In its classical usage, "axiom" signifies an assertion which is adopted without proof, adopted on the authority of the unproven assumption that any contrary opinion must be absurd (whether that assumption is relatively valid or false). For example, a "point" in taught Euclidean geometry is the smallest conceivable image in sense-perception, and a "straight line" is imagined to be, similarly, the shortest distance between two points.

Once these, and other axioms have been adopted as building-blocks for that species of geometrical thinking, no proposition (theorem) adopted must be inconsistent with any among the axioms. Thus, once we adopt any choices of axioms and postulates as a fixed set of underlying assumptions for any formal system, not only will every proposition generated within that system be consistent with each and all of those assumptions, but, each and every proposition which could ever exist within that system is implicitly stated in advance. This principle of formal systems, including all formal systems of mathematics, is sometimes known as the "hereditary principle" of a formal logic such as that of Russell and Whitehead's *Principia Mathematica.*

Since the formal aspect of the economic systems of Adam Smith, Karl Marx, and John Von Neumann each and all claimed to be logically consistent formal systems, this rule, the so-called "hereditary principle," applies to each and all of them. This brings into play a second formal principle of all logical systems, the so-

EIRNS/Carlos de Hoyos

A model for the investigation of conic sections, at the Franklin Institute of Technology in Philadelphia. Geometrical thinking is the axiomatic starting point for correct methodology in economics.

called principle of "types." By treating each of these economic systems as sub-types of a common type, we are able to identify the cause of the presently ongoing, worldwide economic collapse in a simple and direct way.

For our purposes here, the following definition of that principle of types will be sufficient.

Once we show that each and all theorems possible within any logically consistent formal system are all embodied implicitly in a single "hereditary principle," we can replace a listing of such theorems by simply stating that hereditary principle. To construct such a statement, we must present the set of interdependent axioms as a principle for generating, in some ordered or other succession, each and every theorem implicitly possible within that succession.

This leads us to an important, fundamental discovery first elaborated by Georg Cantor. This discovery was echoed by a Twentieth-century mathematician, Kurt Gödel. Gödel, by reconstructing a crucial feature of Cantor's proof, discredited the most fundamental

mathematical axioms of not only Bertrand Russell, but also of the putative father of modern economic systems analysis, John Von Neumann. Leave the related Cantor topics of non-denumerable sequences and power sets untreated here today; the point relevant to our treatment of Smith, Marx, and Von Neumann, here, is fairly summed up as follows.

As Plato demonstrated this famous ontological paradox by his *Parmenides* dialogue: that unifying conception of change which, as a generating principle, subsumes and thus bounds all of the members of a collection cannot be itself a member of that collection. This was demonstrated in a fresh way by Cantor, a demonstration which Cantor situated explicitly in terms of Plato's work, and which Cantor developed as a revolution respecting both the formal and ontological features of all possible mathematical thinking. Thus, if we state the "hereditary principle" of any formal system, such as today's generally accepted university classroom mathematics, in its proper form as a generating principle, that statement lies outside the formal system of elements which it defines implicitly. That fact lies outside the reach of comprehension by today's generally accepted mathematical thinking; but that principle is nonetheless intelligible, knowable.

The history of mathematics itself illustrates this point. The kind of mathematics which may be derived from the kind of set of axioms and postulates presented as Euclidean geometry, yields a form of mathematics called "algebra," or "algebraic systems." That is the kind of mathematics we associate with René Descartes or Isaac Newton. Over the interval 1440-1697, a higher form of non-algebraic mathematics was established, presented in this form at the latter date chiefly by Gottfried Leibniz and Jean Bernoulli. The higher form of non-algebraic mathematics came to be known as the domain of transcendental functions. The Euclidean axioms of point and line were discarded as axioms, and replaced by isoperimetric, or circular action, also known as a principle of "universal least action." The establishment of non-algebraic mathematics as superior to algebraic forms, was demonstrated by the astonishingly accurate, 1670s measurement of the speed of light by Ole Roemer, and by the successive application of this measurement to principles of refraction by Christian Huyghens, Leibniz, and Jean Bernoulli.

Although Leibniz and his friends discredited the axiomatics of algebraic thinking, they took away nothing of importance to science. All of the valid features of algebra are understood from the standpoint of non-algebraic mathematics, but free of the fallacies of algebraic thinking. It is shown that non-algebraic mathematics bounds algebra externally, but that, true to the paradox of Plato's *Parmenides*, the truth of non-algebraic mathematics cannot be derived by construction from a formal algebra. In the language of Cantor, algebraic and non-algebraic mathematical formalisms are two distinct species of "hereditary principle," or, distinct *types*, of which all valid propositions in algebra belong to a sub-type under non-algebraic functions. Similarly, Cantor showed the existence of a third, higher type of mathematics, beyond denumerable arrays, which is a higher type than any variety of today's generally accepted classroom mathematics.

The notion of (transfinite) axiomatic types applies to the problem under investigation here. The systems represented by the mathematically representable features of the political economy of Adam Smith, David Ricardo, Karl Marx, and John Stuart Mill belong to a common, Cantorian type of linear schema which is characteristically entropic, as, notably, Ludwig Boltzmann defines entropy in mechanistic models of a gas system, or any analogous system. The same is true of the systems analysis of John Von Neumann.

The fact that Boltzmann's model is axiomatically entropic leads directly to the following paradox. If the universe as a whole were subject to a universal law of entropy, as Boltzmann's mechanistic model implies, then Boltzmann himself could never have come into existence to construct his theory. Thus, if Boltzmann's theory is valid, then both Boltzmann and his theory never existed.

A scholarly defender of Boltzmann's work would raise an objection to our use of that paradox which is more or less the same point made by Boltzmann himself. That objection would be, that Boltzmann himself showed that non-entropic phenomena might conceivably exist locally within a universe which is overall entropic.

The rebuttal to this objection is, summarily, that such a defense of Boltzmann depends absolutely upon Boltzmann's own reliance upon choosing an incompetent definition of "negative entropy (negentropy)." For Boltzmann to have come into existence, he must be a living process which is capable of progressive, and efficient intellectual discoveries analogous in form to an evolutionary model of living processes as a whole, and also analogous to such inorganic forms of evolutionary self-transformation of a process as the generative principle, or type represented by the developed form of the Mendeleyev Periodic Table of elements and isotopes. As an existing person, Boltzmann, despite his theories, did conform to such an evolutionary model. However, these evolutionary "models," including Boltzmann himself, are not represented by the way in which the purely mechanistic notion of "negative entropy" is defined mathematically by Boltzmann's theorem.

The claim by Norbert Wiener, for example, that Boltzmann's mechanistic model is a model of a principle of living processes, for example, is a plain chicanery. By the time Wiener wrote his *Cybernetics*, there was a well-established, rigorous distinction between the two types of systems, entropic and not-entropic; the formal history of this distinction began with Plato's treatment of the implications of the regular solids' unique construction. In modern science, Plato's argument is developed further by Luca Pacioli, Leonardo da Vinci, and is a central feature of the work of Johannes Kepler. The work of Plato, da Vinci, and Kepler is re-grounded on the basis of Leibniz's *analysis situs* and important later work in this direction by Gauss, et al.; the refinement of Mendeleyev's Periodic Table by earlier Twentieth-century work, up through the 1930s, in nuclear radiation, fusion and fission, made clear what we ought to signify empirically and mathematically by our obligation to make a strict formal distinction between living and entropic processes. The attachment of the word "negative entropy (negentropy)," as a simple time-reversal of statistical entropy, to the non-entropic features of living processes was therefore childish word-play; and Wiener's application of the Boltzmann statistical theorem to define a common principle of human communication and living processes a patent sophistry, a hoax.

In physical economy, for example, negative entropy is properly represented in the following way.

The total consumption of combined infrastructural, producers and households' market-baskets of essential physical goods corresponds to a magnitude which modern practice commonly terms "energy of the system." The desired increase of the total output of production over the "energy of the system" previously embodied in the productive process, corresponds functionally to the relative "free energy" of that society as a process. The ratio of this "free energy" to that "energy of the system," is a correlative of the productivity of that society considered as a whole. Follow this several steps further.

These magnitudes are considered in totality, but they are also considered functionally per capita, per household, per square kilometer, and per square kilometer per capita. In the successful cases, the increase in productivity lessens the per-capita amount of productive effort required to satisfy the maintenance of the required level of the energy of the system per capita. However, there are two other outstanding changes which are included among those required to sustain this rise in the ratio of free energy to energy of the system. As measured in physical, but not labor-time terms, the energy of the system per capita must increase. Similarly, the ratio of total infrastructure goods plus producers' goods, to households' goods, must also increase, although the absolute, physical magnitude of the content of the household's per-capita market-basket must increase. The satisfaction of those preconditions provides a model of what "negative entropy" must signify if we are to attribute to that term any degree of congruence with the distinctively anti-entropic characteristics of living processes. This model illustrates the required alternative definition of "negative entropy" if that term is intended to reference the distinguishing characteristic of any process which would have permitted Boltzmann himself to have come into existence.

This is also the model which an economic process must satisfy to generate a genuine margin of what Marx termed "surplus value," of profit to humanity as a whole. In the case of Adam Smith, David Ricardo, Karl Marx, John Stuart Mill, William Jevons, and John Von Neumann, the systematic formalities of their respective arguments all share the same axiomatic blunder central to both Boltzmann's and Wiener's mistaken mathematical definition of "negative entropy." They are each and all intrinsically zero-growth models, which, as policy-guides, would ensure axiomatically an entropic collapse of any economy foolish enough to tolerate them.

Smith Versus the Physiocrats

We are now situated to examine the way in which the zero-growth axioms were embedded in the work of Smith, Marx, Von Neumann, et al. Briefly, then, as follows.

The science of political economy was developed originally by Gottfried Leibniz over the interval 1672-1716. The Physiocrats, and Smith, Marx, Mill, and Von Neumann after them were all adversaries of Leibniz in science generally, and in the field of political economy in particular. As economists, Smith, Marx, Mill, and Von Neumann were all philosophical adversaries of Leibniz from the standpoint of John Locke; Locke's model of society is key to understanding the common axiomatic fallacies of their economic systems.

The outstanding features of Leibniz's discoveries in physical economy included, first, his development of the notion of heat-powered machinery, and, second, his notion of technology. The first bears upon the increase of the average productive powers of labor of society as a whole through the use of heat-powered machinery. The second involves that increase in productive powers of labor which follow introduction of a principle of design of experimental apparatus of scientific discovery to tools, product-design, and machinery of production, all to such included effect that the per-capita physical productivity of society were increased by this means even without an increase in the throughput of heat-power per capita.

An alliance of certain aristocratic and financial-oligarchical forces mobilized to eradicate the influence of Leibniz's science of physical economy. The most important of these, until about 1783, were the so-called Physiocrats. Later, beginning 1763, during the rising political power in Britain, William Petty, the Second Earl of Shelburne, adopted Adam Smith as an an agent of the opium-smuggling and slave-trading British East India Company, assigning Smith to study the work of the French and Swiss Physiocrats, to design a scheme for destroying the economies of both France and the English-speaking colonies in North America. Smith's apology for the British East India Company's morally objectionable practices, *The Wealth of Nations*, appeared as a Shelburne-backed anti-American tract in 1776. Smith plagiarized significantly the written work of leading French Physiocrats, such as Turgot, but also included the added, pernicious dogma, intended to destroy the economies of France and English-speaking North America, "free trade." Smith, Ricardo, Marx, Mill, Von Neumann, et al., are each and all direct outgrowths of the John Locke axiomatic model of political economy proffered by the British East India Company's Adam Smith.

In contrast, the U.S. Declaration of Independence was based upon Leibniz's "pursuit of happiness," in opposition to Locke's "pursuit of property." Similarly, what became known worldwide as the anti-British

American System of Political-Economy was set into motion under President George Washington through U.S. Treasury Secretary Alexander Hamilton's Leibnizian *On the Subject of Manufactures,* and the thorough complementary credit and national-banking policies set forth in Hamilton's reports to the U.S. Congress on credit and a national bank. The Leibnizian system of political economy, as the form of the future U.S. economy's success was described prophetically by Hamilton then, did correspond to a truly negentropic model, contrary to the entropic schemes of Smith, Marx, Von Neumann, and Norbert Wiener.

Of all of these anti-Leibniz economic dogmas, only the Physiocrats allowed a true profit to society as a whole, and that in a most eerie form. For Smith, Ricardo, Marx, Mill, and Von Neumann, profit is something gained by one person out of the pocket of another, as trading profit, as usury, or some outright speculative swindle such as today's "junk bonds." In Von Neumann's language, for them, as for today's malthusians, economy is a giant, all-seasons gambling hall, an "n-person, zero-sum game." By contrast, the Physiocrats argued that all net growth of the wealth of society per capita is generated solely as the "bounty of nature," not man's productive labor. Implicitly, these French rural oligarchs were pagan worshippers of the Delphi Apollo cult's earth-mother and whore goddess, Gaia. The Physiocrats' favorite prostitute, Gaia, produced all gain in wealth; labor were merely as cattle grazing in Gaia's field, munching upon Gaia's bounty. The landlord, by owning a piece of land, had the only legitimate title to Gaia's bounty, like the man who had rented the pleasure to an hour of Gaia's services as a prostitute.

The human species is known to have lived on this planet for no less than about 2 million years. It appears, that about that time and later, our species had a planetary potential population-density of less than 10 million individual persons, about the potential of a creature resembling the baboon in every respect but man's inferior strength and fighting capacity. Had mankind been merely an animal, mankind today would still live in no more than those numbers and with approximately the same table manners. The characteristic of those changes in potential population-density which have brought us to this time is an increase in both standard of living and productivity expressed in both per-capita and per-square-kilometer terms. This Cantorian type of increase in potential population-density is rooted in those mental capacities of the individual human person which permit mankind to generate and to assimilate efficiently those axiomatic-revolutionary discoveries in science and fine arts through which man's per-capita power over nature is increased.

In respect to any formal system, such as generally accepted classroom mathematics, an axiomatic-revolutionary discovery appears as an absolute mathematical discontinuity.[1] Animal and human behavior must be contrasted axiomatically in these terms of reference.

It would be an exaggeration, to say that the range of behavior of an animal species is delimited in a way which corresponds neatly to a notion of the formal logician's "hereditary principle." We can say, that members of animal species cannot transmit axiomatic-revolutionary forms of discoveries, as conceptions, from one generation of that species, to the next. It appears that, in sharp contrast to the human species, an animal species cannot willfully improve its behavior in the way the radiation of an individual person's scientific discovery of an axiomatic-revolutionary quality is the cause of a revolutionary advancement of the potential population-density of the human species.

Although "animal intelligence" does not correspond simply, ontologically, or otherwise to any system of formal logic, animals lack that principle of intelligent behavior which otherwise sets intelligent behavior apart from, far above any formalist's view of today's generally accepted classroom mathematics. "Animal intelligence" manifestly shares one quality with formal

---

1. Cut one line with another. If we make the second of those lines sufficiently thin, can it become the case that the length of the first line coinciding with the second will be a point on the first line for which there is no denumerable determination of exact position? "Yes," says Cantor's demonstration. This issue was already featured in such locations as Bernhard Riemann's 1854 Habilitation Dissertation; the model of the problem was introduced by Richard Dedekind. It was central in the work of Cantor's teacher, Karl Weierstrass. This is a true mathematical discontinuity. Asymptotic limits which are true discontinuities are therefore never existing theorems of a continuous function which they bound. For an example of this latter principle, compare B. Riemann's construction of his On the Propagation of Plane Air Waves of Finite Magnitude, published in 1860, in which the central point is this notion of an asymptotic limit as a singularity which is not a theorem of the function which it bounds. Similarly, true axiomatic-revolutionary discoveries are not themselves functions (theorems) of the formal (e.g., mathematical) system which is their putative point of origination. Similarly, a series of such functions, as a Cantorian type, is a quality of function which resides outside all generally accepted classroom mathematics, yet inclusively bounds the latter externally.

EIRNS/Elijah Boyd

Construction of a stellated dodecahedron at a geometry class at the Child o' Mine day care center in Southeast Washington, D.C. "Reaching back ... to recent millennia of European culture, we can trace all that we know of the roots of modern science through early discoveries in geometry, such as the Pythagorean theorem, Eudoxus's principle of exhaustion, and Plato's treatment of the regular polyhedral solids."

logic; it excludes ontologically the distinguishing, creative characteristic of human reason.

Human knowledge up to the present day is the continuing elaboration of an accumulation of successive, axiomatic-revolutionary discoveries over perhaps as far back as 2 million years. Reaching back less distantly, to recent millennia of European culture, we can trace all that we know of the roots of modern science through early discoveries in geometry, such as the Pythagorean theorem, Eudoxus's principle of exhaustion, and Plato's treatment of the regular polyhedral solids. With less exactness, but with essential certainty, we can trace back certain features of this development of science to times and places long before Classical Greece, chiefly through the development of solar astronomical calendars: before 6,000 B.C. by channels of the Vedic culture of Central Asia, through such channels as Egypt before the pyramids, and also from the ancient roots of China's culture, perhaps earlier than 15,000 years ago. In general, we can prove geometrically that each step among even those more remote discoveries required an axiomatic discontinuity with respect to any attempted formal representation of a preceding state of knowledge. We also know that such discoveries have an implicit, although not neces-

sarily denumerable successive ordering, an ordering determined by the notion of necessary predecessor.

We have shown earlier in other published locations a similar, philological and physiological case for the rational development of European Classical music, for example, from the vocalized poetry of many thousands of years ago, through the necessary, most recent development of Classical polyphony by Haydn, Mozart, and Beethoven: all on the foundation of earlier development of Florentine methods of *bel canto* voice-training and of J.S. Bach's more immediate well-tempered revolution in counterpoint.

To grasp adequately this principle of axiomatic-revolutionary discovery, otherwise termed "Platonic hypothesis," we must rise above the popular myth of so-called "scientific objectivity," to the higher vantage-point of "scientific subjectivity." This is the place in the present report to supply the following interpolation.

Science as Classical Poetry

Contrary to prevailing opinion among today's professionals, and also contrary to today's popular opinion, the "secret," if you will, for accessing true human knowledge was presented in a fresh way by Georg Cantor's treatment of the transfinite. At this point in our report, that principle of knowledge is located by "triangulation" of three points of reference: Cantor's principle of transfinite *types*, Cantor's direct comparison of that principle of the higher mathematics with Plato's treatment of the relationship between the *Becoming* and the *Good*, and a comparison of Cantor's work and Plato's method with the inner artistic principle of composition of Classical tragedy. We now describe that summarily, as follows.

In each of those three facets of today's accumulated human knowledge, and in all taken together, we see that, relative to any attempted formalist representation of knowledge, that knowledge exists in no such formalism, but rather in no less than that Cantorian type of principle by which each and all successive phases of man's progress are ordered. To sum up this point in the

Hale Observatories

A spiral galaxy in Ursa Major (32 NGC 5457). "Perhaps we shall not reach deeply enough into the interior of the atomic nucleus until we have completed the appropriately corresponding work of exploration of space."

simplest admissible terms: In contrast to a formalism, such as today's generally accepted classroom mathematics, knowledge is not symbolic, but is premised upon a process of successive axiomatic-revolutionary discoveries. Knowledge lies not in any among those successive discoveries as individual elements of a series, nor in an formal construction derived from a collection of such elements. In contrast to the formalist standpoint, knowledge appears as a succession of those "mathematical discontinuities" which mark the formally impassable boundaries separating the lower form of knowledge from the higher.

These boundaries, these singularities are bridgeable only by that principle of discovery under which Plato subsumes commonly the distinctions among hypothesis (discovery), higher hypothesis (principle of successive discoveries, or type of discovery), and hypothesizing the higher hypothesis (the ordering of revolutionary improvements in method of discovery).

As a matter of contrasts, modern empiricism is formally *reductionist*. It seeks to find the smallest, ostensibly indivisible element of matter, to the purpose of defining the universe as a whole inductively, by building upon the assumedly most elementary relationship among the most elementary building-blocks of matter. As that reductionist method is exemplified formally in the extreme by Bertrand Russell and Alfred North Whitehead's *Principia Mathematica*, such radical empiricists or positivists adopt the same fallacy met in today's popularized neo-malthusian foolishness of "non-parametric" statistics: the absurdity of seeking a substitute for causality within the empty expanses of bare linear space-time.

On the contrary, the ontological principle illustrated by Plato's *Parmenides* obliges science to seek knowledge by ascending to that inclusive whole which is not comprehensible as a member of the set which it externally bounds and defines. In a sense, we must find the pathways to the secrets of microphysics in astrophysics; perhaps we shall not reach deeply enough into the interior of the atomic nucleus until we have completed the appropriately corresponding work of exploration of space. We must find the lawful basis for causal determination of the relationship among parts in the principles of ordering of the universe in the astrophysical very-large.

It is relevant, that the most ancient known roots of modern physical science may be found, tens of thousands of years ago, in the solar astronomical, long-cycle calendars of Central Asia from which historical Indo-European and Chinese civilizations sprang. Coming nearer to today, we have similar evidence of the development of solar astronomical calendars in Egypt long before the great Pyramids were designed. According to such ancient evidence, even before historic times, any culture which lacked a calendar of more than 26,000 years, based on a sound conception of sidereal and solar cycles, was pathetically poor in its relative cultural development.

It is indispensable that we seek knowledge in the highest rank of the largest conceivable wholes, not the smallest part; but that is not sufficiently rigorous, by itself. We must examine the accumulation of human knowledge by means of a constant criticism of our own thinking-processes at each stage of generating, regenerating, and transmitting scientific knowledge. In each successive phase of this process, we must attain a higher level of conscious reasoning by adopting the relatively lower levels of our own thinking as the sensuous-like objects of consciousness. This is the method of Plato's Socrates, of ferreting out and rendering intelligible the often hidden, often provably false axiomatic assumptions which underlie carelessly a tolerated blind faith in that received as authoritative opinion.

What else could be a more useful method today? Virtually all governments have been ruining the planet over decades, by tolerating generally accepted academic opinions on economics, opinions which have all long-since proven themselves, by events, to have been virtually a global mass-suicide pact among nations.

It is not sufficient to accept the fact, that we must achieve conscious control of those blind assumptions which govern the tongues of the illiterate Ph.D.s, and of others today. To render this Platonic method, and its terminology, truly intelligible, Plato himself would have considered it quite proper that we imagine this Socratic process as like a classical tragedy being performed before a theater audience. After all, are not his dialogues written as dramas? The players are performing the script on stage. The audience is watching the minds of each of the characters on stage, and the playwright, seated in a box above both stage and audience, is watching the minds of the members of the audience, and thus seeing his own mind's activity more clearly in that way.

Let it be said, in memory of Plato, Dante Alighieri, Leonardo da Vinci, Rafael Sanzio, Johannes Kepler, and Gottfried Leibniz, that without a mastery of the Classical fine arts, there can be no true physical science. Without rejecting the irrationalist, romanticist aesthetics of Immanuel Kant, the skills of the physical scientist dwell in but a small imperilled oasis within a Dionysiac wilderness of a Wagnerian opera, within the irrationalist, romantic mind of a raving, existentialist beast. Unless the leaders in physical science reject Kant and Friedrich Karl Savigny's barbaric dichotomy of *Naturwissenschaft* (natural science) and *Geisteswissenschaft* (art), unless they reject contemptuously the existentialist lunacy of "art for art's sake," physical science as a whole tends to become sterile; powers of creativity are lost, and only the soulless formalities of a no longer creative, dead science remain, until even that, too, is rotted away. "The play's the thing, to catch the conscience of the king"; in the great Classical tragedies of Aeschylus, Miguel Cervantes, William Shakespeare, and Friedrich Schiller, the doors to the innermost secrets of creativity in natural science are opened for the sake of those willing to enter. Imagine the tragedy as a Plato dialogue, and discern the structure of that dialogue to parallel Cantor's exploration of higher reaches of the transfinite.

Imagine that that play we chose to watch, follows the practice of such classic Platonic tragedies as Cervantes's celebrated prose-drama *Don Quixote,* in which the characters within the tragedy step briefly out of their roles to address the audience in soliloquies. These soliloquies have the effect of a character's showing his or her awareness of the audience; but, there is a certain ambiguity about this: Is the player speaking to the audience in his capacity as the character portrayed, or as the actor playing that part? As the audience is watching the drama, the drama is looking into the mind of the audience; this is the case at the same time that the soliloquist is presenting a view of the state of mind of the characters within the ongoing drama.

The common essential of all these relations, within the performance of the author's drama before an audience, is conscious viewing of consciousness as were that latter consciousness itself a sensuous object. The audience is watching the consciousness of the characters portrayed, as it is prompted to do so by such devices as Shakespeare's or Cervantes's soliloquist. The playwright is focused upon the conscious processes *within the minds of the members of the audience*. In a great tragedy, such as the *Prometheus* of Aeschylus, the tragedies of Shakespeare, and, most clearly of all, of Schiller, the interplay inhering in one consciousness being treated as an object by another consciousness is a truly Socratic dialectic.

All true human knowledge is Socratic in that sense. We touch knowledge as we rise above the beasts, as we rise above the empiricist's folly of knowing no objects but his blind faith in his felt reaction to the object-images of his sense-experience. Knowledge begins as we shift our attention away from his faith in his sense-perceptions, as we begin to search out the hidden, axiomatic assumptions which permeate and control the way in which we judge our own, and others' conscious processes of judgment, of opinion-making. Knowledge begins as we explore the implications of making indispensable modifications of those previously hidden assumptions which we are able to uncover, those axiomatic beliefs earlier hidden from our awareness.

Thus, great drama, especially the great classical tragedy reflected by such as Aeschylus, Shakespeare, and Schiller, is a wonderful, health-giving stimulus, a taking of pleasure in scientific rigor. Merely accepting a taught formal mathematics, is learning, not knowledge. As both the known and hidden axiomatic assumptions of all mathematics are treated as conscious processes, which are, in turn, properly objects of conscious criticism, that joyous experience which is truth-seeking knowledge begins.

This dramatically Socratic criticism of assumptions is no merely arbitrary negation. This point is conveniently illustrated by recognizing that Cantor's discoveries are a reflection of that same method of exhaustion we meet in the work of Plato and Archimedes, for example. The principle of solution in the case of Plato's *Parmenides* ontological paradox, as Cantor and Kurt Gödel have addressed this successively, is key to understanding the way in which the method of exhaustion succeeds. Briefly, we have the following.

Given, the recent 2,500-odd years of known history of civilization, and of education: The formal side of the proper education of the child, for knowledge instead of today's slap-dash, behavioristic learning, comes into focus near the onset of adolescence, with the study of classical geometry, and a concurrently included study of Classical Greek culture from the reference-point of Plato's dialogues. In contrast to such stupefying empiricists as Peretto Pomponazzi, Francis Bacon, John Locke, David Hume, and so forth, Plato aids the student in overcoming the bestiality of blind faith in sense-experience as such. Viewing Classical Greece through the eyes of Plato, one sees that knowledge begins by rising above contemplation of blind faith in sense-experience, to examining the states of consciousness associated with judging sense-experience.

The method of judging is typified by Eudoxus's principle of limits. Drive every assumption to its limits, seeking out the way in which the ontological paradoxes, of the type presented in Plato's *Parmenides*, are forced into consciousness. So, the higher (than empiricist) state of consciousness associated with Platonic *hypothesis* is made a subject of consciousness. Our awareness of a state of consciousness of *hypothesis* as a Cantorian type, is consciousness of *higher hypothesis*, and so on. Thus, the secrets of physical scientific discovery are embodied in great dramatic tragedies.

The limit which situates the hypothesis of axiomatic-revolutionary discovery, is always as Plato's *Parmenides* defines it. This is the definition illustrated by Nicolaus of Cusa's revolutionary solution to Archimedes's formulation of the paradoxical chore of squaring the circle. By leaping directly to the outer limit of a process of generating ever-more many-sided, regular, inscribed and circumscribed polygons, it is shown that such an increasingly precise method for estimating a numerical value of π could never bring congruence between the perimeters of the polygon and that of the circle. The two are of different species, the principle of *circular action* the superior species bounding "externally" the process of generating the polygons.

In that circa A.D. 1440 discovery by Cusa, we have the axiomatic germ of Leibniz and Jean Bernoulli's demonstration of a non-algebraic form of universal least action. Similarly, Carl Gauss's derivation of his *pentagramma mirificum* from examination of the principles of Keplerian regular and semi-regular partition of the internal surface of a spherical shell, is a fresh insight into the nature of the Golden Section in respect to the Platonic solids, not as a coefficient in Galileo's dynamics, but as an external bounding of a geometrical process driven to its limit.

Cusa's discovery of the absolute distinction between a circle and *circular action*, the germ of modern transcendental functions, is taken as an intelligible example of the principle of hypothesis. Grasp that discovery in terms of the type of generating principle to which it belongs; reach thus an intelligible representation of the notion of Platonic higher hypothesis. Once the preconditions for Cantor's work are seen in this kind of classical-tragic dramatic setting, as prompted by the relevant paradoxes treated earlier by Gauss, P.G. Lejeune Dirichlet, Berhnard Riemann, and Karl Weierstrass, the students' consciousness is lifted above the chimeras of naive denumerability, and the once awesome face of hypothesizing the higher hypothesis assumes friendly, intelligible form.

Cantor's writings reflect his own experience with such discoveries. Yet, more stunning at fresh encounter then than even all the reflection upon the role of hypothesis in scientific discovery, is the re-reading of Philo *On Creationism*, and the Christian writers on the interrelated topics of *imago Dei* and *capax Dei*. Acknowledge Plato's conceptual distinctions between "Becoming" and "Good," as Cantor insists that these parallel his own distinctions between "transfinite" and "absolute"; see then the meaning of *imago Dei* and *capax Dei* as that species-nature of the individual person which, according to Genesis 1:25-28, sets mankind absolutely above all other existence within a temporal universe.

Contrary to the beliefs of empiricists like (left to right) Jeremy Bentham, Karl Marx, and John Von Neumann, the historical increase in mankind's potential population-density sets man apart from and above all other creatures, and defines individual persons as in the image of the Creator.

Man's ability to replicate the behavior of Aristotle and Bertrand Russell's formal logic, we can simulate by a mere machine designed to handle such ontologically trivial matters as simultaneous linear inequalities. Poor Aristotle, poor Immanuel Kant, poor G.W.F. Hegel, poor Russell; one must wonder if they are not condemned to reside in Dante's Inferno forever, their tantalizing punishment that of being instructed monotonously throughout eternity in "the practical reason" by one of poor John Von Neumann's machines! Their crime, for which they might be punished so appropriately, is that their evil life's work was devoted to preventing their dupes from discovering the beauty of what it can be to be human.

The form of the interdependent qualities of *imago Dei* and *capax Dei* is reflected uniquely in that quality of supra-formalist creative reasoning which is directly illustrated in valid axiomatic-revolutionary discoveries in science, and in analogous discoveries in the Classical forms of the fine arts. From the standpoint of making ourselves conscious of the successively higher layers of our own capacity for scientific and artistic thinking, we recognize hypothesis, if but negatively, at the paradoxical, Eudoxian limit typified by Plato's *Parmenides* and Cusa's *De Docta Ignorantia* and *De Circuli Quadratura*. We recognize creativity, in its form as hypothesis, as the formal discontinuity implicit in any axiomatic-revolutionary form of discovery.

With those considerations of scientific progress as a subject of Classical tragedy in view, now view the conflict among Leibniz, the Physiocrats, and the British free traders as such a tragedy.

The Tragedy of Empiricism

The essential falsehood, the lie upon which the teaching of the Physiocrats, Adam Smith, Jeremy Bentham, Karl Marx, John Stuart Mill, and John Von Neumann is commonly premised, is the same lie about mankind for which Aristotle, Kant, Hegel, and Russell might be justly tantalized forever in Dante's Inferno. Contrary to such persons, that historical increase in mankind's potential population-density which sets mankind apart from and above all other creatures within temporal eternity, defines individual persons as in the imperfect image of the Creator. This is so by virtue of manifest powers of axiomatic-revolutionary forms of efficient creative powers: in Latin, the powers of *imago Dei* and *capax Dei*.

One of the subjects of this report is, that those customary pagan Gaia-worshippers, the Physiocrats, deny such creative powers to man. It is appropriate that the core of these Physiocrats was provided by a political union of feudal landlords and financial usurers, like the North American defenders of the institution of chattel slavery. In the opinion of such worshippers of that old whore of Babylon earth-mother, it is a capital crime of *hubris* to attribute the image of the Creator to that mere serf, or slave for whom they would care no more, perhaps less than the cattle they compassionately fatten for slaughter.

Adam Smith's employers were a late-Eighteenth-century variety of British Liberals, radical empiricists. Therein lies the nub and source of their differences with the Physiocrats.

The Physiocrats, together with their allies among the banker usurers, were defending their traditionally greedy bucolic's forms of feudal oligarchism, defending their usurious social customs, so to speak, against the encroaching social, economic, and political outgrowths of the fifteenth century's, Florence-centered Golden Renaissance.

The radical empiricists Earl of Shelburne and Jeremy Bentham exhibited the point of conflict with the Physiocrats, as they, from London, directed the Jacobin Terror of their agents Orléans, Robespierre, Danton, and Marat against France. The British East India Company's radicals were the Physiocrats' allies against the heritage of the 1439-40 Council of Florence, but were unwilling to subordinate their rapacious utilitarianism, their neo-Roman lusting for world empire, to the restraining force of any form of social custom, even that their sometime feudal Physiocrat allies. So, later, did Lord Palmerston's "Young Europe" revolutions of 1848-49 treat Britain's faithful allies Metternich, the czar of Russia, and the king of France most ungratefully.

Formally, there are two essential differences between the empiricists and the best spokesmen among the Physiocrats, Quesnay and Turgot. First, the best Physiocrats have a clear sense of the structure, if not the functional characteristics of the productive process, where the empiricists, from Smith through John Stuart Mill and Jevons, never have. It is essentially on this single count of Marx's debt to Quesnay that he is superior as an economist to his Haileybury predecessors, and to the modern monetarists. Secondly, the leading Physiocrats believe in the existence of a net social profit to society as a whole, whereas the empiricists do not. Although Marx the economist is superior to Smith and David Ricardo on one point, he is otherwise, mathematically, the faithful follower of Bentham and Ricardo. That said, we have situated ourselves to concentrate upon the formal side of empiricist economics.

The key to a mathematical reading of the economic dogmas of Smith, Bentham, Thomas Malthus, Ricardo, Marx, and Mill is the social doctrine of John Locke. In Locke's system, society is merely the aggregation of a large number of discrete, neo-Aristotelian particles,

people, into an interacting, polymorphous tangle defined essentially by the consideration that each of these particles is motivated by nothing more than three primary impulses: to stay alive (Life), to pursue sensual gratifications (Liberty), and greed (Property). For Locke, there are no "innate ideas." Excepting a lively, utterly amoral libertarian zest for greed, the individual is born a "blank slate" (*tabula rasa*). This, Locke's definition of "human nature," serves as the axiomatic basis for the "hedonistic calculus" of Bentham, and, later, the radical-positivism "systems analysis" doctrine of Von Neumann et al.

Each and all of the formal systems presented by Smith, Marx, et al. demand no more sophisticated a form of mathematics than a system of simultaneous linear inequalities. Marx's would not be as crude a model as Von Neumann prescribed, but there is nothing essential in *Capital* which is not implicitly encompassed by such a general system. For this reason, the mathematical form of the ideas of each of these political economists, from Smith and Marx, through Von Neumann and his followers, produces a zero-growth model. Perhaps what we have just said on the distinctions and kinships of Marx and John Von Neumann was in the minds of Cambridge's Joan Robinson and Nicholas Kaldor, as they blended portions of Marx, John Maynard Keynes, and Von Neumann to cook a poisonous Cambridge proprietary "systems analysis" stew for export into the International Institute of Applied Systems Analysis's (IIASA) Moscow.

The crux of these connections is, that systems representable in the form of simultaneous linear inequalities describe only "zero-growth systems," or, more precisely, entropic processes. Consequently, to the degree a successful effort is maintained to regulate any physical process according to the specifications of such a mathematical system, that physical process will have imposed upon it in this way a negentropic form of degeneration. We should add the corollary observation, that even processes which are not otherwise inherently entropic will, if so controlled, either slowly degenerate in this way, if they do not abort such control by collapsing outrightly.

Under these conditions, a policy-shaping system which describes mathematically an entropic process, if used to control a society, will drive any society so controlled to entropic collapse. That is the key to the ongoing spiral of collapse of both the former Soviet and the Anglo-American systems.

Pioneers in the development of thermodynamics (left to right): Leonardo da Vinci, Christian Huyghens, and Gottfried Leibniz. "There, in those revolutionary impulses of the creative processes of mind, not in the empty space-time of algebra, lies the efficient cause for the not-entropic form of development of successful economies."

3.0
Negentropic Processes

The essential lesson which all literate persons must learn from the presently ongoing collapse of the global economy as a whole, is that whenever a physical process, such as an economic process, is efficiently regulated by ideas whose mathematical representation is entropic, the result will be a collapse of whatever process was effectively regulated in this way. Thus, we have indicated that the efficient, increasingly strict imposition of the ideas of John Locke, of Adam Smith, et al. upon more and more of the world's economy, is the leading cause for the want and chaos spreading throughout the United States and the world as a whole during the recent quarter-century.

To this effect, we have indicated already that the attempt to express the political economy of Adam Smith, Karl Marx, John Von Neumann, et al. in a form suited for administration of economic affairs, such as accounting, imposes an entropic collapse upon any economic process efficiently regulated in this way. We have emphasized that all possible mathematical descriptions of any among the British and derived dogmas in political economy, that of Marx's *Capital* included, has the in-

herently entropic characteristic more nakedly presented by Von Neumann's (zero-sum) systems of simultaneous linear inequalities. They are each and all, in fact, zero-growth models; therefore, they are each and all entropic models.

We have also indicated that, although the leading Physiocrats did recognize the possibility of a net physical profit to society as a whole, they denied that the generation of such a physical profit could be induced originally by willful human intervention.

We have indicated that real economic growth must be compared with such evolutionary models as our biosphere, or that implicit in such a view of our universe's generation of that array of elements and isotopes presented by the Periodic Table. We have stressed, that this "model" is certainly not entropic, but neither is it merely "negentropic" in the sense that the work of Ludwig Boltzmann, Norbert Wiener et al. define "negative entropy." Any consistent apologist for Boltzmann would be obliged to emphasize, more or less readily, that Boltzmann allowed the occurrence of reversed entropy only within the limits of what Von Neumann termed a "zero-sum game" for economy.

All of those British and derived models of political economy which are found in the pantheon of "Economics 101" are dangerously absurd, in that sense that any economy efficiently regulated by them must suffer a general collapse. Emphatically, any national or global economy tightly administered on behalf of present-day "neo-conservative" ideas of "democracy and free-trade," or of so-called "International Monetary Fund conditionalities," is doomed to collapse into a state of economic and political disintegration, into chaos.

We have also noted, in contrast to that dismal side of the matter, that the human race has exhibited some notable successes in political economy. We have risen from a species endowed naturally with cultural potentials at the level of baboons, from a potential living population of not more than approximately 10 million, short-lived persons, to a present global potential, at present levels of existing technologies, of about 25 billion and rising. We have taken the first steps toward the feasibility of not merely exploring, but colonizing nearby space. We have increased vastly the productive power and feasible standard of living and average life-expectancy in regions of the world economy which have access to the benefits of investment in scientific and technological progress. Such evidence of long-range, quasi-evolutionary forms of upward social development of systems of political economy is what we understood during 1945-63, for example, as the kind of referent which defined modern civilized use of the term "economic growth."

Although the causal principle of this progress cannot be represented in any existing form of generally accepted classroom mathematics, there are crucial adumbrated features of this process which, although anomalous in mathematical-physical implications, we may define more or less readily in terms which admit of representation as mathematically comprehensible forms of physical constraints. Those crucial adumbrated constraints show us that the process so reflected is absolutely not entropic. Although these constraints define an ordering which does not fit within the axiomatic assumptions underlying the so-called three laws of Clausius-Kelvin thermodynamics, that ostensibly anomalous characteristic is precisely what must be represented. That representation suffices to show that the proper descriptive term for this anomaly is not "negative entropy," but the more modest term "not entropic."

This anomaly does not represent a reversal of entropy, but rather a completely different ordering of the relevant processes.

This anomalous form of the process parallels the similarly anomalous forms of living processes. Thus, we may say, that as the Classical Greeks of Athens carved their geometrical way of thinking about life in Acropolis stone, and as Nicolaus of Cusa, Luca Pacioli, Leonardo da Vinci, Kepler, et al. have presented this case during the past five and a half centuries of the existence of modern science, living processes are certainly not characterized by a statistical notion of "negative entropy," but are better described as simply "not entropic."

Consider the following, interpolated summary of the way in which a simplified, but indicative set of such constraints is built up for statistical comparisons.

As we have indicated above, the set of constraints which shows this anomaly must be derived from an expression of mankind's practical relationship to the universe as a whole. Obviously, since man's relationship to the universe is currently expressed in terms of Earth's location within our solar system, all these relations are reflected in mankind's habitation upon the planet's surface: per square kilometer. The functions of production and consumption, and correlated functions, of survival (reproduction) of the human race are expressed thus in per-capita values. Since the individual's demographic existence is a function of the family household, we must reflect this, too. We have, thus: total, per capita, per household, per square kilometer.

Man's activity on this account is represented chiefly as a correlative of *physical* production and consumption. The only forms of *services* which are closely correlated with those physical features, are education, professional medical care, science, and classical forms of the fine arts of poetry, drama, music, painting, sculpture, and architecture. However, the requirements for these forms of *services* are implicit in the cultural levels underlying sustainable successive increases in per-capita and per-square-kilometer physical productivity.

So, the indicative parameter of the reproductive relationship between the universe and mankind as a whole, is the Cantorian *type* of process represented by this view of humanity's consumption of its own production. This kind of "input-output" relationship is the pivot for an adumbrated notion of statistically representable "function." This undertaking is broadly analogous to squaring the circle. In the latter case, as treated by Nicolaus of Cusa, the attempted squaring provides a linear approximation of the value of π, whereas the use of the method of exhaustion to show an absolute species-difference between the polygonal and circular perimeter forces the mind to recognize the superior ontological actuality of substituting non-algebraic *circular action* axiomatically for the naive Euclidean axiomatics of point and straight line.

The analytical key datum for defining this function, is the ironical relationship between the physical quantity of contents represented by the per-capita household or producer's market-basket and the number of labor force working-years of production per capita required to produce that per-capita market-basket of consumption. This market-basket, in turn, is correlated with the relative cultural level of physical productivity per capita, per household, and per square kilometer. The physical constraints immediately associated with these ironical input-output relationships form the keystone for building the required statistical representations.

The first approximation made to this purpose, is the definition of *productivity*.

The first term of the general function for statistical representation of productivity is: The content of the physical market-basket must be improved in quantity and quality over successive intervals, but the proportion of the per-capita working year required to produce that improved market-basket must be less than the proportion required formerly to produce the old.

The second term of the same general function, is the ratio of per-capita expenditure for producers' goods, relative to households goods must increase, without lowering the per-capita households' goods market-baskets. This reflects the necessity for increasing "capital-intensity."

The third term of that same pivotal function, is the requirement of an increase in the ratio of "free energy" to "energy of the system." For this purpose, free energy signifies the increase of total market-basket physical value produced with respect to total market-basket physical value consumed. This margin of increase is absorbed chiefly twofoldly: in expanding the scale of the physical economy, and in increasing the capital-intensity of investment in production. These gains must be expressible not only in terms of production as such, but also physical values per square kilometer, per capita, and per household.

This type of function is obviously anomalous mathematically. Nonetheless, it describes the relevant statistical appearance of those qualities of phenomena which accord with successful economic growth; also, it describes the statistical reflection of actual processes conforming to successful growth of physical economies. Although other constraints must be considered in a fuller statistical treatment, the kernel of the anomaly is situated within this set of axiomatically pivotal terms of the function as a whole. This typifies the statistical appearance of the constraints adumbrated by a "not-entropic" process.

This pivotal, core set of interlocking constraints is closely associated with central features of Leibniz's representation of a physical economy based upon the principles of heat-powered machinery. Firstly, it was Leibniz's initial objective to provide mankind with the benefits of the fact that one man, employing a heat-powered machine, could accomplish the work of 100 others not so equipped: Broadly, a "not-entropic" form of rise in productive powers of labor requires a trend of increase of both the quantity per capita and the "energy-flux density" of power supplies. Secondly, it requires a coordinate advance of the level of technology. Also, the quantity of usable qualities of water, for both personal and other essential consumption available per capita, per square kilometer, per day must increase. The ton-miles of freight moved per hour, per square kilometer, and per capita must increase, and the relative physical cost of moving a ton-mile must decrease. The relative duration, facilities for, and intensity of that type of leisure devoted to science and classical forms of fine arts must increase, to foster thus the extent and rate of development of the creative powers of the individual mind.

Within the constraints of systems analysis, for example, such a set of constraints could not be satisfied. Wherein lies the paradox?

It is the same paradox referenced by Isaac Newton, in warning the reader against the tendency of his *Principia* to paint the universe in the color of what we call "entropy" today, a universe which could not exist were God not to wind it up periodically. That is the same Newton "Clockwinder" paradox famously referenced by Leibniz in the book of Leibniz-Clarke-Newton correspondence. The fact that we can locate within a set of statistical constraints a type of result which cannot appear in systems analysis ought not to be considered surprising, unless a mathematician were committing an all-too-common elementary blunder of the positivist, the naive ontological blunder of attributing the quality of causality to the space-time gaps of an algebraic function.

The function of the mathematics of denumerable orderings is to map space-time relations, not to attribute to space-time itself the causal principle governing the physical processes situated in that space-time. If we do not make that crude ontological blunder, we are at liberty to describe statistically either entropic or not-entropic relations; if we commit that ontological blunder, we fall into the "Clockwinder" paradox of which both Newton and Leibniz spoke so famously nearly 300 years ago.

Unfortunately, to the degree mathematical training lays more or less primary emphasis upon algebraic thinking, rather than that of Gaspard Monge and Jakob Steiner's improvements in geometrical thinking, it is much easier for the student to lose that mooring of mathematical sanity which is a constructive geometry. The student who depends too naively upon algebraic methods, may lose a developed sense that algebraic thinking, at its best, represents pictures painted in mere space-time, which is never to be mistaken for the higher domain, the real domain, of physical space-time.

I think that nothing could expose this problem, and its implied solution more clearly than the science of physical economy.

The set of interlocking constraints we have described just above, describes the form of a not-entropic process in a special choice of phase-space, that shadow of the actual process being examined. Within those chosen limitations of the description used, that is the *form* of the transformation described by the constrAints. What is the *content* of the same transformation? What are those causal features of the transformation which exist outside the domain of mathematical formalism as such?

The efficient cause is the mind of man, those processes of relatively more or less developed powers of creativity which are the source of the generation, transmission, and assimilation of ideas which represent a valid, axiomatic-revolutionary transformation in previously established opinion.

By their very nature, such ideas of discovery cannot be represented mathematically, nor communicated explicitly by any form of language. Relative to any established formal system of representation, an axiomatic-revolutionary discovery is an absolute discontinuity, for which no consistent representation is possible. However, one man, the discoverer, may prompt the reoccurrence of that act of discovery in another person, by presenting effectively the paradox—the failure of the hearer's previously existing formal knowledge to be able to comprehend a relatively anomalous, hence, "paradoxical," phenomenon.

This form of communication is identified as belonging to the class of metaphor. Axiomatic-revolutionary discoveries cannot be communicated within the medium of previously existing forms of a language. They can be communicated only by employing the methods of paradox to generate a metaphorical, indirect form of artistic communication, by activating within the hearer the creative mental processes which are capable of replicating the creative-mental act of axiomatic discovery being described metaphorically by the speaker.

The form of not-entropic growth of economy which we have identified here is a result of the reorganization of human productive and related practice under the influence of scientific or analogous forms of beneficial, axiomatic-revolutionary discoveries. Although it is important that we understand the development of science and fine arts from the earliest knowable portions of our species' past, during most of the the recent six centuries of European history, until approximately 1967-74, there has occurred a general rate of growth of per-capita and per-square-kilometer productivity, beyond any precedent in the known evidence of the existence of the human species during the preceding 2 million years. This is associated with a correlated pace and intensity of revolutionary discovery in physical science and the Classical forms of fine arts beyond compare, in known preceding times.

Although there has been a generally accelerating collapse in literacy and the extent of Classical fine arts practice during the course of this century, especially during the recent 30 years, we have reached the condition that to maintain acceptable rates of progress in economy, we must devote up to 5% or more of the total employment of the labor force of leading nations to the generation and development of new technologies as such, in science and engineering.

Axiomatically, the implications of the recent centuries development of science-driven industrial society are but a continuation, albeit with qualitatively greatly intensified force, of what was always true for mankind. Nonetheless, the transformation of the required structure of the total labor force's employment over the recent 600 years, from over 90% rural as recently as the U.S. census of 1790, to less than 2% required directly today, and the growth of increasingly capital-intensive, energy-intensive urban manufacturing, with the latter's large science-driver requirement, has brought us to the verge of the colonization of locations within what science has redefined for us as relatively nearby space.

The margin of the population required to be employed specifically in generating both fundamental scientific and technological progress, has thus grown from the relative scale of Plato's Academy at Athens, to a number of household-members supported by science and technology which would be greater than our total population of this planet 600 years ago. We have not yet reached those required levels of such employment, but the requirement itself, approximately 10% of the world's total population, is none the less indicative of the quality of change which has occurred over the preceding six centuries.

Unless this planet collapses into a prolonged "New Dark Age" about the onset of the new century immediately awaiting us, the tasks of physical economic recovery will have obliged us to move, at an accelerating rate, in the direction of virtually a purely science-driver form of global economy. Under such conditions, it is an intelligible prospect that, within several generations, more than half of the world's labor force might be employed in developing the ever-more productive technology which the remainder of the labor force requires.

This is a transformation which began during the Fifteenth Century, centered then in Italy, around such central figures as Filippo Brunelleschi, Nicolaus of Cusa, the Paolo del Pozzo Toscanelli who constructed the map used by Christopher Columbus, Luca Pacioli, and Leonardo da Vinci. This is the outcome of the design of the industrial revolution based upon heat-powered machinery, a revolution already foreseen and designed during the Seventeenth Century by the Christian Huyghens who pioneered the piston engine using explosive fuels, and the Leibniz who shaped the development and application of the coal-fired steam engine.

There, in those revolutionary impulses of the creative processes of mind, not in the empty space-time of algebra, lies the efficient cause for the not-entropic form of development of successful economies. The constraints of that not-entropic economic process represent the preconditions which society must mobilize itself to fulfill, if that form of development is to be achieved. In effect, the form of not-entropic result defined by those constraints informs us, who must cause this to occur, that we must be willing to incur certain relative amounts of cost for certain essentials, such as science-driver, capital-intensity, educational, health, and power-intensity elements, or fail to realize those not-entropic goals. It is not the mathematician's empty space-time, but we, with our creative powers of mind, who are the cause of not-entropic forms of economic growth.

3.1 The Politics of Growth

The political implications of the Fifteenth-century Golden Renaissance ought to be implicit for anyone who examines the prophetic quality of U.S. Treasury Secretary Alexander Hamilton's 1791 Report to the Congress *On the Subject of Manufactures*.

Leibniz cautioned that heat-powered machinery, such as the successful steam-engine designed by his collaborator Denis Papin, should be applied initially with an emphasis upon the improvement of mining. Then, the improvement of the extraction of coal in increasing amounts and cheapness appropriate to general requirements of heat-powered machinery was a precondition for the general application of heat-powered machinery. Hamilton, following Leibniz's conceptions, showed how the use of the "artificial labor" of powered machinery could be used to develop urban industries, while at the same time reducing the percentile of the population employed in agriculture, but increasing the per-hectare yield of farming above that earlier.

This transformation requires a relatively high quality of universal compulsory education of young children and adolescents. This must be a training which qualifies the young in general scientific principles, as a rigorous training in geometry grounds such capabilities, since the required character of employment will require included emphasis upon the assimilation of technologies derived from new discoveries.

If we educate the young accordingly, we produce a population which knows that all men and women possess that potential for creative reasoning which marks them, each and all, as in the living image of the Creator. Such a population will be inclined to accept, as useful to all, the practical recognition of development of relatively greater merit in some other person, but will resist the notion that inherited name or wealth constitute the members of a social class or caste morally better than themselves. The kind of world populated almost entirely by well-educated plebeians of that republican disposition is not a happy prospect for the classes of parasites whose wealth and power depend upon financial speculation and kindred forms of usury.

For the sake of Life, Liberty, and Property as empiricist John Locke defined these, the oligarchs prefer the charms of serfdom's bucolic imbecility, and a hard-working, low-paid, simple sort of general urban population. The oligarch's utopia is a world in which the young are taught desirable attitudes, but not compelled to assume their duties of any fully free and mature human being, to assume responsibility for such knowledge as classroom development of the individual's cognitive powers for geometry, Classical fine arts, and knowing also the intrinsic intelligibility of that kind of a world of work and everyday family life which is dominated by the impact of the physical sciences.

For as long as history records such matters, and as the sundry kinds of surviving shards of the archeological record confirm this for pre-historic periods, the essential, global political conflict dominating all general and individual human life, has been: Which kind of a world shall we have, the oligarch's world in which scientific and technological progress is suppressed to the purpose that the overwhelming majority of people are kept as stupefied, manipulable brutes, or a world designed to fit the requirements of individual persons in the image of the Creator?

British "free trade" dogmas were developed by the self-styled "Venetian Party" of Britain, the oligarchical party. Those dogmas were formulated at the behest of "Venetian Party" leader Shelburne beginning at the time, 1763, Britain had broken the maritime power of France. This victory allowed Britain to achieve worldwide what Venice had earlier achieved as the pivot of its imperial power throughout the Mediterranean—absolute supremacy in sea-power. During that same post-1763 period, Shelburne and his lackey Bentham launched Edward Gibbon into production of his celebrated *Rise and Fall of the Roman Empire*: Britain's Liberal Party, the formal name for the "Venetian Party," intended to establish a British worldwide empire in fact, establishing London as the global capital of a "Third Rome." As Britain's brutalization of its colonial subjects attests, Britain's global utopia was a world in which most peoples of the planet were kept ignorant, barefoot, and pregnant, but, by aid of disease and famine, not populous.

Britain has become almost a worldwide empire, even though the British Isles have become a post-industrial rust-bucket, large portions of its population reduced to the status of Yahoos, and its military power

EIRNS/Philip Ulanowsky

Standing guard at Whitehall. "As Britain's brutalization of its colonial subjects attests, Britain's global utopia was a world in which most peoples of the planet were kept ignorant, barefoot, and pregnant, but, by aid of disease and famine, not populous."

scarcely even a symbol of its former potency. It dominates the world not as a nation, a people, but through the nearly unchallenged hegemony, in all national capitals of the planet, of an empiricist's axiomatic assumptions of policy-shaping.

Today's British world-empire does not fly the Union Jack. The old red coats of uniformed tyranny are no longer visible. Today, the empire exists in the more easily managed form of a multicultural human zoo, in which each nationality or ethnic grouping thus victimized is pitted against all others in that Hobbes form of conflict which Kant termed "heteronomic." Although the special belief of the respective tribes are mutually exclusive in this sense, each and all of this multicultural array of cult-dogmas is premised upon the underlying set of empiricist axioms as all others. Thus, each nationality is a gamepiece operating according to rules of the game embedded in each and all by the British ideological gamemaster. In the same way, each is a theme-park creature in a human game-preserve for which British empiricism is the gamekeeper.

This same imperial function of British empiricism extends to the domain of political economy, into the fine arts, and into the domain of physical science.

From the middle of the Seventeenth Century until about 1827, the anti-Descartes, and anti-Newton factions in France represented virtually unmatched world leadership in science and in technology. From about 1827 through World War I, the standard of competence in both education and physical science was Germany. The neo-Newtonians were brought into prominence in France by order of the victors at the 1814-15 Congress of Vienna, as the leaders of France's world supremacy in science at that time, Lazare Carnot and his teacher Gaspard Monge, were expelled: Carnot was sent into exile, in Germany, and Monge was expelled, together with his program of education, from the Ecole Polytechnique which he had built. It was the power of the victors of the 1815 Vienna Congress and the British house of Welf-Hanover, which imposed anti-Leibnizian, British empiricism's ideological influences, Kantian forms of romanticist irrationalism, Hegel, and Savigny upon post-1815 Germany.

Similarly, it was Britain's participation in the victors' role at the close of World Wars I and II, as in the Congress of Vienna earlier, which has made British empiricism hegemonic in law, in political economy, and the ideology of physical science throughout most of the world today.

None of this was done to the advantage of the British population—poor wretches that most of them are today. It was done for the sake of a parasitical form of oligarchical financial system which inhabits the United Kingdom, not as a citizen, but a succubus. As we dumb-down the cattle we breed for meat and milk, so the British imperial succubus dumbs-down the breed of human victims which it breeds and exploits like mere cattle. To accomplish this, it is not sufficient merely to destroy the victims' minds with "outcome-based education"; it is also necessary to remove from the economic process that factor of technological improvement of quality of goods and of productivity of labor, which depends upon fostering the cognitive powers of the mind of child and adolescent.

So, these succubus-imperialists of the Anglo-Saxon oligarchy treat all mankind as cattle, by turning all humanity into a Giuseppe Mazzini-style, multicultural zoo, one theme-park's ideology more imbecilic than the other. What is forbidden, above all, is to teach children and adolescents the form of scientific literacy which can be achieved only by shifting emphasis away from the schizophrenia of formal proofs to replicating in one's own mind the acts of axiomatic-revolutionary discovery of the exemplary greatest discoverers in all known history before this time. That prohibition, that state of mind comparable to the fertility of the eunuch, is what is called empiricism.

4.0 Economics as the Only Science

The preceding successive phases of this presentation have prepared us to now introduce observations which many readers will find the most shocking of all. At least, that will be a rather common initial reaction. We shall present the argument supporting the following such conclusion: *that all valid human knowledge rests upon demonstrations found empirically within the domain of physical economy.* As a first step, situate that proposition within those outlines of a *theory of knowledge (epistemology)* which are implicit in our arguments here thus far.

Thus far, we have indicated six levels of human knowledge, the five lower among which are accessible in intelligible form as human knowledge. These may be represented in the following order of ascending rank:

1) The lowest, nearest to bestial level: sense-perception, naive, usually irrational reaction to experience.

2) Formal knowledge, as cohering with the notion of judgment of experience by means of an axiomatically "hereditary principle."

3) Individual, valid, axiomatic-revolutionary discovery, overturning a body of formal knowledge: *hypothesis.*

4) An ordering-principle, or cantorian *type*, generating a succession of valid hypotheses: *higher hypothesis.*

5) The notion of an in-some-sense orderable ranking of differing qualities of *higher hypothesis: hypothesizing the higher hypothesis.*

6) Implicit certainty of the existence of a higher, non-temporal order subsuming hypothesizing of the higher hypothesis, as higher hypothesis subsumes hypothesis: Plato's *The Good,* and Cantor's *absolute.*

On the premise of the argument elaborated during the preceding pages of this report, we focus attention upon a more restricted part of this epistemologist's array, the three Platonic "levels" of hypothesizing. Now that we have listed the six levels of what might be regarded as the range of knowledge, we limit our use of the terms "knowledge," or "human knowledge," to signify the products of a more or less successful use of consciousness of the intelligibility of the three levels of hypothesizing.

For the case of simple *hypothesis*, the first, and simplest, of the three levels of hypothesizing, the implicit relationship to an increase in physical productivity, per capita and per square kilometer, was adequately indicated earlier here.

For the second case, *higher hypothesis*, consider one specific *type* of such a scientific method of discovery.

EIRNS/Stuart Lewis

Lyndon LaRouche (second from left) receives the diploma of his election in October 1993, to the International Ecological Academy of Russia. He received the diploma at the Feb. 18-21 Schiller Institute conference in Washington, D.C. It was presented by Taras Vasilievich Muranivsky (left) and Prof. Wolter Manusadjan (right), vice president and president, respectively, of the academy. LaRouche is joined by his wife, Helga Zepp-LaRouche. This article is the fuller elaboration of the speech he gave at that conference.

For this case, employ Eudoxus' method of exhaustion, as used by Plato, Archimedes, and Cusa, among others. Reference, as a model of the use of this method in generation of hypothesis, the cases of Plato's *Parmenides* dialogue and of Cusa's application of Plato's *Parmenides* paradox to solve the paradox of Archimedean quadrature. This signifies, implicitly, that every proposition to be tested for an included paradox should be reduced to its constructive-geometric form of representation, and that representation then driven, by the method of exhaustion, to beyond its limits. The existence of a geometrically defined ontological "species gap" between that function and some asymptotic boundary, at that limit, defines the relevant paradox.

Hypotheses defined by aid of employment of this method constitute a *type,* a type which corresponds to a specific way of generating a series of higher hypotheses, an *higher hypothesis.*

In geometry generally, there is another, distinct principle, also used by Plato, and by Johannes Kepler and Karl Gauss, among others. It may be used in conjunction with the method of exhaustion, but represents

a distinct type of generative principle. This may be described as "the quantum field principle," as illustrated by the use of a geometrically ordered distribution of singularities by Kepler to determine the available orbits and their harmonic relations, or the seemingly "magical numbers" prompted to our attention by Dmitri Mendeleyev's discovery of the Periodic Law of chemistry.

The second is closely related to a third principle, pertaining to the differences in ordering subsumed by the distinction between positive and negative curvatures. This was stressed by Kepler, but was already treated implicitly by Plato's "quantum field" treatment of the dodecahedron and Golden Section.

Each of these available choices of generative principles may be employed, singly, to generate the quality of ontological paradox implying an hypothesis. Also, for example, the first two might be employed in combination. The more numerous the valid such generative principles so employed, the greater the formal power of the resulting type of higher hypothesis. This comparison is an obvious choice of example of *hypothesizing the higher hypothesis*, as adumbrated for representation here.

This imagery leads us to recognition that the sole source for certainty and intelligibility within the totality of human knowledge is a view of physical economy which corresponds to such notions of hypothesizing. This is the epistemological consideration which implicitly underlies a competent science of physical economy.

As Genesis I specifies man's given power and corresponding responsibility to be the master of this temporal universe, so mankind must measure its relationship to that universe.

This injunction of Genesis I is proven to be no unintelligible command, as if to be carried out in blind faith by the obedient.

It is a fully intelligible instruction, thus a knowable truth fully binding professed heathens, too. This certainty is imposed upon all rational persons, as we are able to demonstrate absolutely the manner in which individual man's power of creative reason sets mankind apart from and above all other existences within this temporal universe. It is therefore the intelligible principle which Gottfried Leibniz recognized as *natural law*. This is the basis for the lawful authority of a universal morality, as even the professed heathen must recognize this to be the case.

As man must give an accounting for the behavior both of his species and of himself individually, so must we constantly judge our society, and ourselves, in every facet of our activity and existence. This, reason instructs us that we must do according to such implicit, and specific requirements of universal natural law.

That use of the term "accountability" may be seen as interchangeable with the properly defined term "knowledge." That signifies *knowledge of mankind's relationship to the temporal universe.* That also signifies, for each of us, our individual relationship to the process of influencing the relationship to this universe of our nation as a whole, of mankind as a whole. That means, that there can be no true knowledge without such a sense of accountability for mankind as a whole, as that sense is imparted to us by the power of creative reason.

That means, therefore, *knowledge of hypothesis.* That means, therefore, *knowledge of hypothesizing.* That means, therefore, *knowledge of hypothesizing the higher hypothesis.* That requires, therefore, knowledge of some yardstick, by means of which principle of ranking the internal ordering of the process of hypothesizing the higher hypothesis may be rendered efficiently, morally intelligible.

Example: Today's Global Crisis

Up to the point of this concluding section of the report, we have emphasized the approach by means of which the correlation between scientific progress and increase of mankind's standard of living and potential population density may be rendered efficiently intelligible for guiding education and other indispensable policy-shaping practices. We have situated that aspect of the subject-matter, physical economy, in respect to a presently ongoing, global collapse, a seemingly unstoppable collapse into a looming void of global "new barbarism," a void which is the extinction of all civilization as we have known it.

Let us underscore a few, perhaps pedagogically indispensable, illustrative points from among this crisis's painfully embarrassing personal implications for many ordinary citizens of various nations.

That looming smell of something akin to Apocalypse does not permit us to limit blame for the world's presently worsening misery to accusing a relative handful of politicians, or some analogous scapegoat. The problems before us are not the result of "mistakes"; the failure of policy-shaping which presently grips the entire planet is of a systemic, global, and axiomatic quality. The evidence presented by this crisis, is that the human race, virtually in its entirety, has failed; the existing body of generally accepted public opinion, in all nations, at every level of society, and of virtually all persons, has caused this present crisis.

The fact that we might attribute "blame," in the sense that we can show how this matrix of pathological opinion came to rule virtually all of this planet, top-down, does not permit the use of the term "innocent by virtue of ignorance" to excuse the unwitting citizen. That citizen may indeed have adopted destructive forms of popular, and populist opinion out of blind ignorance and pathetic suggestibility; but, his support, even his mere toleration of such dogma, has contributed to allowing the crime against all humanity which those beliefs have brought about.

If one is driving an automobile to destruction under the influence of intoxicants, one gains no escape from the laws of nature by pleading momentary ignorance. If one chooses to believe that "free trade" is the naturally superior policy of all humanity, and millions of people in some foreign country die of hunger and disease because of the imposition of "free trade" upon that region of the world, you who support that idea have guilty complicity in the suffering and death of those millions.

That person is fully as guilty personally as the drunken driver who kills a pedestrian.

The intended thrust and relevance of this argument is the following. If a catastrophe to society is brought about by the deliberations of a few, using principles unknown, or not tolerated by, the majority of the society, then the error of opinion which must be corrected should be designated accordingly. However, if the disaster is caused by application of beliefs which have been generally supported, or even merely tolerated by, the majority of adult opinion, then the majority of that nation is to be blamed. We must say, under such a circumstance, that the condition cannot be cured without exposing the criminal disposition inhering in the relevant aspects of the prevailing public opinion of that nation's majority. So, today, for example, everyone who supports those immoral ideas called "free trade" is guiltily complicit in respect to the ongoing destruction of civilization as a whole.

That illustrates in part what we signify by our use of the term "systemic."

Those of us who stand as candidates for election, or have visible claims to expertise of some sort or another, are constantly confronted with the question: "What is your alternative?" respecting this or that proposed or existing policy. In respect to the effects of today's "free trade" dogmas, my own answer to a demand that I politely propose "alternatives," rather than denounce, is: "When you make the demand, 'What is my alternative?' I tell you that you are being dishonest; you are evading the implications of the issue which you find morally demanding upon yourself. If I see a man sexually abusing a child in the street, and someone asks me, 'What alternative do you have to suggest to that man?' I would react in the same way as I do to the evasiveness of your diversionary question now." When a murderous or suicidal policy is axiomatically wrong, it is immoral to demand any alternative to promptly defying, uprooting, and destroying that axiom of belief.

For example, the evasive question: "Destroy 'free trade'? What, then?" In the case of the United States, for example, the mere elimination of "free trade" means a "relapse" into the wonderfully successful "protectionist," anti-John Locke, anti-Adam Smith, Leibnizian principles reflected in Article I of the U.S. Constitution, and U.S. Treasury Secretary Alexander Hamilton's, and also Friedrich List's explication of those principles. One does not require a documentary proposal of new alternatives to remove a fish-bone from the throat.

Whence comes the global influence of those ideas which are responsible for the self-destruction which threatens imminently all nations and peoples, including the United States, today? To this point, it could be proven beyond intelligent rebuttal, that the spread of the ideas of John Locke, through the political victories of the British Empire since 1763, has established the selection of those popularized ideas whose influence is responsible for the ongoing global collapse today. This includes, as examples of that phenomenon of influence, former British colonies, which have established their nominal political freedom, but which administer their own nations "quite independently" under the influence of ideas premised axiomatically upon the multicultural principles of British empiricism.

Yet, halt there for a moment. Look at that post-industrial rust-bucket which is today's post-Harold Wilson, post-Margaret Thatcher Britain. With that set of facts before one's eyes, could anyone be so naive as to insist that the ruin of the world has been conducted to the advantage of the Celtic-Anglo-Saxon population of the United Kingdom, the ordinary British person's ingathering of Locke's Life, Liberty, and Property? Yes, the hallmark of the global self-destruction in progress is the spread of the influence of British empiricism into places which include India, Argentina, Nigeria, Brazil, and the United States today. It must also be emphasized, as well as merely granted, that this spread of empiricism came through such signal events as London's participation in the victories of 1763, the London-directed Jacobin Terror in France, the 1814 Congress of Vienna, Britain's use of the Russian revolution of 1905 to defeat the policies of Count Sergei Witte, its use of its protégé Adolf Hitler to overthrow the 1933 Kurt von Schleicher government of Germany, and Britain's geopolitical wars against threatened economic cooperation in northern Eurasia, World Wars I and II. That is all true and useful information, but it does not address, and might be misused to divert attention from, the underlying issue posed by the present, systemic global crisis.

The British Empire was not some autochthonous development thrown up by the ranks of the people of England, Wales, Scotland, and Ireland. It was imposed from abroad, by the most powerful force in the Mediterranean of the time, the world-capital of slavery and usury, Venice. During the period from 1582 onwards, London, like Rotterdam, was taken over by the neo-Aristotelianism of Padua, the cultish, hesychastic "spiritualism" of Gasparo Contarini's circles, and the family financier trusts of Venice's *Giovani* faction. These Venetians around the notorious Paolo Sarpi came like a Hollywood filmmaker's "body-snatchers," to take the souls of Englishmen and turn some among them into privileged replicas of Venetian oligarchs. The ideas of these Venetians were essentially a continuation of the pagan Roman pantheon, of the former Greek and Hellenistic center of Mediterranean usury and kookery, the Delphi cult of Apollo, and of the evil usurers and slave-traders of Baal and Moloch before that.

The issue here ought to be more or less readily intelligible. It is not the exertion of physical force by men which rules mankind. Mankind is ruled by the force of ideas, by the interplay of those contending ideas which, acting through the minds of men, thus control the physical conduct of society.

Biologically, there are no intrinsically good or intrinsically bad nationalities; the term "race" is essentially a meaningless one, which would mean nothing but for the regrettably persisting lunacy of belief in race by some deranged creatures. The human race is made up of nothing but individuals who share in common that spark of creative reason which defines all persons as in the image of the Creator. There are only good versus bad ideas; there are some very evil axioms of belief proliferating around this planet still, including bad ideas whose germ is as old as Shakti, Ishtar, Baal, Dionysius, and the old whore Gaia's Apollo Cult of Delphi.

The Venetian "body-snatchers" conquered the general opinion of numerous British institutions, spreading those anti-Renaissance ideas known as empiricism, usury, magic, and racism. This was the foundation for the ideas of such later British radicals as Adam Smith, Jeremy Bentham, John Stuart Mill, John Ruskin, Aleister Crowley, Bertrand Russell, and H.G. Wells, and John Rawlings Rees's London Tavistock Clinic. The now-departed imperial institutions which formerly flew the Union Jack were temporarily the vehicle through which the generally accepted authority of these ideas was spread. The acceptance included, today, the majority of the establishments and textbooks of most nations of this planet.

Those times have passed. Today, Britain's elite has collapsed like old Sodom and Gomorrah. The Nineteenth-century Britain has become an inglorious rubble, a shrunken, pathetically mewling relic of its departed imperial past. The trouble is, the disease spread by that departed empire has a cancerous life of its own. The grip of those entropic Venetian ideas upon the decision-making of governments and international institutions has efficiently ensured that the decisions carried into practice are, at least predominantly, a force for destruction of civilization as a whole.

Example: Today's Official Lies

The evidence of global physical-economic collapse, which we identified in the beginning of this report, is indisputable statistically, and is evident to any mature citizen who compares the bill of consumption of 25 years ago, and the photographs of places from that time, with the corresponding evidence from today. New York City, for example. Yet, we hear repeatedly of recoveries which in fact never occurred; the only evidence which might appear to corroborate those glowing reassurances is the cancerous growth of purely speculative forms of financial liabilities.

The correlated feature of this same recent history, is the record and results of successive, post-1965 changes in policies. Of this one might say, "The more things change, the more they remain the same." Things become worse. The problem is acknowledged, and a reform is promised. A reform is then made. Things become worse. Worse, and then worse, and then worse: So it has gone, from reform, to reform, to reform, for most of the world, for about 30 years. The problem does not lie with any one policy, but with the axiomatic assumptions which underlie the way in which successive reforms in policy are made. The banner upon which such U.S. reforms, always for the worse, have been made, is emblazoned, "Democracy and Free Trade."

Examine briefly the fraudulent way in which the word "democracy" has been employed. For this purpose, focus for a moment on the turning-point in the Civil Rights campaigns of the 1960s.

Until the Rev. Martin Luther King was assassinated, the Civil Rights movement was moving to re-establish those notions of *legal right under natural law* which were engraved in the plain intent of the 1776 Declaration of Independence and 1789 Federal Constitution. If an African-American were denied such rights, then that right did not really exist as a right for anyone; if, on the contrary, anything which African-Americans won as a right, became thus re-established in fact as a right for every person. Then, "bang"; it ended. Immediately, that Spring of 1968, the Ford Foundation of McGeorge Bundy and Dr. Kenneth Clark intervened at Columbia University campus, and elsewhere, to mummify the Civil Rights movement, and replace integration with a new guise for old "Jim Crow," a program of recruitment to an African-American "theme park" in an all-American multi-cultural human zoo.

In Britain, the Labour Party provided socialized medicine, until the private competition was no longer an available alternative, and then the trap was closed upon the victims who had formerly thought themselves beneficiaries. I have no reason to doubt the sincerity of President Lyndon Johnson's support for civil rights; he sponsored a ticket on the train of progress for all Americans, African-Americans included. What happened after Dr. King was assassinated? They went to the ticket-window, they took their tickets, they boarded the train, they found seats awaiting them; but, the train never moved. The railway line had just been closed down by the authors of the newly introduced "post-industrial utopia." Outside that train gathering dust, were the recruiters for the Ford Foundation's segregated, all-African-American theme park, offering recreational drugs to lessen the pain.

That is what the word "democracy" has come to signify in the mouths of the propagandists for "Project Democracy." "Free trade" meant, since 1978, deregulation of transportation, deregulation of banking, and, after 1982, deregulation of those who loot public and private pension funds with "junk bonds."

Those are sufficient illustration of the point to be made. In each case, and the almost limitless number of analogous ones which could have been listed, the problem is located not in the fallacies of a particular law, or other form of policy. The problem is located in the generative assumptions *underlying* each of a succession of policy-reforms; the problem lies in the "hereditary principle" of presently accepted modes of policymaking.

In each case of this type, statistical reporting on the state of the economy, or others, the fault in the standard of measurement for analysis, and the flaws in the type of policy-shaping employed to design reforms, are usually coordinated in character. In economy, as in the example referenced, the flaw is often to substitute nominal values, such as notional valuations of capital in monetary terms, which is a most common cause of statistical hoaxes. Related kinds of axiomatic fallacies are the general rule for most cases.

Any case of this sort may reflect one, or a combination of two, types of fallacy in the policy-shaping assumptions used. Either the axiomatics are disastrously wrong from the beginning, as is true for "free trade," or

a limit has been reached, in which region what was tolerably successful under earlier conditions is no longer tolerable. In these kinds of cases, there is some useful resemblance to the notion of Platonic higher hypothesis, at least in the negative sense. It is the generative principle of faulty policy-shaping which must be altered, axiomatically. Unless that is done, attempts at reform will proceed in no direction but from worse to still worse. The solution is to apply the principle of higher hypothesis.

4.1 Economics and Higher Hypothesis

The increase of mankind's potential population-density is the yardstick to be applied to control the choice of higher hypothesis. For our purposes here, we may approximate "potential population-density" by increases in the physical-economic productive powers of labor, per capita, per household, and per square kilometer. We include implicitly in this education, medical care, scientific research, and engineering services to production, physical distribution, and basic economic infrastructure. This does not include all aspects of required consumption and productivity, but it includes most of the total, and is the most characteristic content of increase of potential population-density generally.

The implied proposition is, that increase of potential population-density, as I have defined it, is in some way a basis for proof of a type of higher hypothesis. Since so-called "fundamental," or, better said, axiomatic-revolutionary discoveries in physical science are the most typical source of increase of the physical productive powers of labor, it is also an implied proposition, that increase of potential population-density provides the metrical standard for judging choice of scientific method. Perhaps this appears an extremely radical claim; put that to one side for the moment. Examine the salient implication of the implications stated thus far.

The spectacle of the hair rising upon the napes of some necks among the science professionals reflects the stubbornness of the widely held, but exaggerated belief among most mathematicians, that proof is mathematical in nature, at least in respect to form. This belief is tolerable as long as the propositions examined in this way are limited in type to those consistent with the "hereditary" axiomatic implications of the form of mathematical repesentation employed. Once an axiomatic-revolutionary proposition is put on the table, the ordinary sort of mathematical proof becomes axiomatically an absurdity; proof of this is identified above.

Although it is presently the conventional view that we must rely upon "inductive" generalizations from formal proofs, once we acknowledge the implications of axiomatic-revolutionary forms of discovery, the fallacy of inductive formalism should be promptly apparent. In the latter case, we must treat the act of discovery itself, formally a "mathematical discontinuity" terminating the competence of the "hereditary principle," as the primary datum.

The latter requirement is not mysterious, provided one has been educated in agreement with the Classical Christian humanist tradition of Gerard Groote's Brothers of the Common Life. As I have been obliged frequently to reference this matter: Such a Classical education rejects the textbook methods for those of replicating the act of discovery reported by original (or proximate) sources. The effect of this method is to accumulate knowledge in the student's mind, each discovery in the form of its replication, as a reliving of the original act, by that student. That student is familiar with the reality of hypothesis, in that way. These moments from some of the greatest minds in all prior history live, as glimpses of the original discoverer's innermost personality, within the mind of the student. Thus, the notion of a principle of discovery is readily accessible to a student who has been educated in this way.

From this standpoint of reference, one can trace readily the nature of the causal sequence linking an original axiomatic-revolutionary discovery to its efficient consequences as increase of the physical productive powers of labor.

Once a discovery has been effected, its efficiency must be demonstrated in what is loosely termed often as "a crucial way," according to strict notions of design of experiment. This was described, among other locations, in the current *Fidelio* (Spring 1994) report on my 1948-52 discoveries in physical economy. The refined crucial experiment serves as a model of reference for introducing a new technology as an included principle of machine-tool design or analogous applications. The transmission of the physical expression of a discovery, in this way, together with the cognitive principle involved, is the source of increases of the physical productivity of labor—per capita, per household, and per square kilometer.

As indicated, a continuation of this process generates a not-entropic form of increase of the ostensible ratio of "free energy" to "energy of the system," as measured in per-capita, etc. terms. This includes the previously stated qualification, that the ratio of producers' goods production to households' goods production increases, although the physical quantity and quality of households' goods consumption, per capita and per household, is increasing, while the per-capita social cost of producing the market-basket is declining. It is this not-entropic form of ordering principle, taken together with its practical implications, which serves as a good approximation of increases in relative potential population-density.

It is the impact of a principle of discovery upon such a desired not-entropic result which is the demonstration of the validity of that form of higher hypothesis. In the corresponding fashion, this is also the referent for hypothesizing the higher hypothesis.

Restated: This view is measuring, so to speak, the relationship between mankind and the universe. This is made in the only way possible; the practical question to be answered, is *whether there is greater or lesser correspondence between the intended production of the preconditions for successful reproduction of the human race, and the laws of the universe which govern the results of those attempts?* The answer to this question is not to be found in fixed ideas, not in ideas premised formally upon a fixed set of axioms, but only in some principle of change of such ideas, from a lesser to greater degree of efficient correspondence with the lawful ordering of our universe. This desired correspondence, through such change, must plainly be measured in no other terms than relative potential population-density.

This is a question to be resolved by resort to some generally accepted classroom mathematics. This is the means by which to discover what is a relatively better or inferior form of mathematics, as the geometric comparison of the algebraic, non-algebraic, and transfinite types of mathematics exemplifies such variety.

In this sense, and no other, the standpoint of physical economy is the fundamental premise for physical-scientific, and also artistic, knowledge. Knowledge itself is man's conscious examination of mankind's conscious powers for generating valid axiomatic-revolutionary hypotheses, for accomplishing that by aid of discovery of a scientific method of successive discoveries, called an higher hypothesis, and for improvements in the quality of such a scientific method, called hypothesizing the higher hypothesis. This is claimed, and nothing more.

Yemen Conflict Misconceptions Refuted

by Kim Sharif

Kim Sharif is Director of Human Rights for Yemen. She refutes the standard misconceptions about the war on Yemen in the clearest terms.

Yemen—A Modern Day Concentration Camp

May 13—In the early hours of March 26, 2015, the children of Yemen say they heard the sounds of massive "fireworks," which they attributed to some sort of national celebration—only to discover later that it was the start of a nightmare of bombardment, starvation, and immense suffering that seems to have no end in sight. Who is doing this and why?

Saudi Arabia, through its then-Ambassador to Washington Jubeir and its spokespe son General Al-Asiri, made an announcement in English and Arabic, claiming that they had formed a coalition of nations including Morocco, Egypt, Jordan, Bahrain, Kuwait, UAE, Qatar, Sudan, Senegal, Pakistan ("the Saudico"), and attacked Yemen in order to restore the so-called legitimate government of Yemen led by former caretaker president Abdrabbuh Mansur Hadi, at his request.

The Saudi-led alliance later added to its claims that its additional aim is to prevent Iranian expansion in the region and to enforce UNSC Resolution 2216. I shall deal with each of these claims separately under its own heading, to see whether there is a grain of truth to what they have been claiming, and to show the consequences of their actions for the people of Yemen.

The Lie about Restoring Hadi

Hadi, the former deputy to former president Ali Abdullah Saleh, was chosen as a caretaker president following the Arab Spring of 2011 in Yemen, to lead the country for a period of two years, during which he was to hold a general election, among other things, under the Gulf Initiative ("the GI").

It should be noted, that as a condition for the validity of the GI, all parties which were involved in the Arab Spring revolution had to agree to it and sign it. Ansarullah (the Huthi and others), Al-Harak (southern separatists) and others have neither agreed to it nor signed it.

The GI came into effect in February 2012 and expired in February 2014, but Hadi had not fulfilled any of its mandates!

We are told that the period of the application of the GI was extended by a further a year by a quango of people appointed to their positions by Mr. Hadi. But that extension itself expired in February 2015. Thus, there was no legitimacy to Mr. Hadi whatsoever, from the start of the GI all the way to its expiry in February 2015.

This therefore makes the attack on Yemen by the Saudico illegal, and all the actions taken by it from March 26, 2015 to date amount to Crimes against Humanity.

Iranian Expansion a Red Herring

The Saudico has claimed later, during its relentless campaign of aerial bombardment of Yemen—using all manner of weapons, including cluster bombs and chemical bombs—that it is doing so in order to prevent Iranian expansion in the region through Iran's alleged proxies—the "Huthis."

In reality, the Huthis are a small minority of Zaydi Yemenis from the northern part of Yemen—Sa'dah—bordering Southern Saudi regions, and members of the Ansarullah Party. U.S. and U.K. officials have countered the Saudico claim of Iranian involvement in the situation in Yemen. One British official, Andrew Mitchell, conservative MP and former Minister for International Development, stated clearly, "We should be wary of demonizing the Houthis and branding them as owned by Iran. They are not."

The fact is, following Mr. Hadi's failure to perform his mandates under the GI, the condition of the country deteriorated to an intolerable level, and by September 2014, a coalition of parties including Ansarullah, the Yemen Army, the Congress Party (the party of former president Ali Abdullah Saleh), Al-Harak, and most tribes and their elders rose and besieged the presidential palace in Sana'a, demanding that Hadi carry out his mandates. Hadi escaped in women's clothing to the Southern city of Aden, where he put together a militia of fighters to support his bid to return to power. Several requests to him to work towards a smooth handover of power failed, when he rejected them outright.

Meanwhile, Ansarullah and its coalition partners, which became known as the Army and Popular Committees ("the APC"), captured the capital, and many other regions fell to its control without much ado. Thus a *de facto* government came into existence in this way, which has now formed the current government of Sana'a under Yemen's constitution, with a fully functioning parliament. Under the UN Charter, this is the government of the sovereign state of Yemen, which must be recognized under international law.

Several fronts of armed confrontation then erupted, led by renegade generals of pro-Hadi militias in the areas of Ta'iz, Mokha, Aden, Ma'rib, Al-Jowf, and Nahm. The APC later withdrew from the South, which has ever since been under occupation by foreign UAE forces aided by terrorists and mercenaries. Many are reporting untold horrors in the South. In some parts of Ta'iz, pro-Hadi militias have committed genocide against the tribes of Al-Rummaymah and Al-Junaid in a manner identical to Da'esh practices of crucifixion, skinning people alive, and mutilating their bodies. The leaders of these pro-Hadi terror militias are Wahhabi takfiri leaders Hammoud Al-Mikhlafi (currently in Turkey) and another one called Abul-Abbas.

At the head of the renegade generals is Ali Mohsin Al-Ahmer. This general belongs to the Party of Islah (the Muslim Brotherhood of Yemen), and was in charge of recruitment of mujahideen during the Afghan-Soviet war in the 1980s. He is also behind Al-

Qaeda in the Arab Peninsula (AQAP) in Yemen, and thus also Da'esh. In fact, there is ample evidence to show that the Saudico fighters are fighting alongside these terror outfits. What connects the two is ideology, the Wahhabi takfiri ideology—and, of course, petrodollars.

The Islah Party's spiritual leader is Sheikh Abdelhameed Zandani. Zandani was placed on the most-wanted list for terror offences by the U.S. authorities, and is currently hosted in Riyadh. Hadi is its political leader, and general Al-Ahmer its military leader. The Nobel Peace Prize-winner Tawakul Karman is one of its celebrated soldiers—she was one of the agitators of the Arab Spring in 2011. Hammoud Al-Mikhlafi and Abul-Abbas are among its followers.

The Saudico also engaged the services of both the notorious Blackwater and Dyne Corporation, which brought mercenaries from other countries, such as Colombia, Mexico, Australia, and even the UK and Israel. Not a single Iranian national has ever been found to have a hand in the Yemen war. However, many other groups, including terror outfits, have been found fighting alongside the Saudico.

On the Saudico claim that they are enforcing UNSC Resolution 2216, it should first be noted that laws cannot be retroactive. That is, if we can call the Resolution "law." First, it was passed some three weeks *after the start of the bombardment of Yemen*—on April 15, 2015—and it cannot retrospectively legitimize an act of war against a sovereign state. Second, there is nothing in the resolution allowing any military measures, as the Russians have pointed out. Third, the Security Council is not a lawmaker itself—rather, it is subject to the laws of the UN. Fourth, no instrument of the UN can ever be used to commit War Crimes, Genocide or Crimes against Humanity. Therefore, it is a total fallacy for the Saudico to rely on this instrument at any time.

Modern-Day Concentration Camp

According to UNICEF, a child under the age of five dies every ten minutes in Yemen due to malnutrition. This equates to approximately 60,000 deaths of children a year in Yemen due the actions of the Saudico, as they are enforcing a strict blockade, preventing the entry of vital food and medicine into the country through the only functioning port, the Port of Hodeidah.

The Saudico admitted nearly a month ago that it had carried out up to *90,000 airstrikes* on Yemen during

the last two years! This admission should have made the international community aghast, and resulted in a demand for the immediate cessation of hostilities against Yemen, particularly in light of the fact that the country is facing famine. According to UN reports, up to seven million people in Yemen are food insecure—at best, struggling to avoid hunger.

The situation was made much worse when the Central Bank of Yemen was moved from San'a to Aden by Hadi, and up to 4 trillion rial of notes printed in Russia were handed to Hadi's team. The Central Bank now cannot supply the necessary import credits for the food immediately needed.

General Asiri admitted in an interview with BBC, that they are taking these measures in order to prevent "Huthis" from gaining power in the country. In other words, the starvation of the people of Yemen and the use of all manner of lethal weapons, is being done with the sole intention of killing them if the people of Yemen refuse to obey the Saudis and insist on supporting Ansarullah—as they do, for millions of people have flocked to the capital city of Sana'a to demonstrate in support of the current government there.

The majority of the Saudico airstrikes have been carried out against civilian targets, and the country's entire infrastructure has been destroyed. Nothing has been spared: schools, universities, hospitals, homes, sports facilities, food stores, farms, factories, heritage sites, mosques, airports, seaports, and much more. Figures show that up to 15,000 civilians have killed and over 50,000 injured. These figures don't include the children who die as a result of malnutrition. Thus, it is right to say that Yemen is a modern-day concentration camp and a killing field for the Saudico.

Author Kim Sherif, addressing a demonstration in London.

Any strike on a civilian target, even if it is later discovered that the target was used for military purposes, amounts to a War Crime under the Geneva Convention. Thousands of War Crimes have been committed against Yemen by the Saudico. The UN can't even commission an independent investigation into the matter, but, much to our horror, the UN now rewards the Saudis by giving them a place at the UN Human Rights Council and Women's Rights committee!

While the killing continues, the international community is stricken with a shameful silence and inaction. Furthermore, they continue to insist on forcing everyone to accept Hadi's quango in Riyadh as the legitimate government, even when they know that Hadi's grouping—which has become known as the government of "Facebook" due to its lack of popular support in North and South Yemen—have nil legitimacy, and are fighting alongside terror outfits. All of Yemen's embassies, which are the property of the state of Yemen, are under *de facto* illegal occupation by the Qataris who are paying the salaries of the staff, and support the Islah Party. All staff are Muslim Brotherhood followers. Qatar is the biggest supporter of the Brotherhood internationally.

This war is an act of aggression illegally executed, leading to thousands of deaths and total destruction of the country, while millions are facing imminent slow, horrible death by starvation and lack of medication. Failure to intervene to stop this war will be an ugly scar on the international community, and nothing will heal its ugliness.

Kim Sharif made the following presentations to the United Nations Human Rights Commission: https://www.youtube.com/watch?v=ZIoijDOPx3M

www.ingramcontent.com/pod-product-compliance
Lightning Source LLC
Chambersburg PA
CBHW081152280526

45787CB00008B/3298